The Essence

of

MERTIE WILLIGAR BUCKMAN

Trish Calvert, Ph.D.
Edited by Ilene Jones~Cornwell

Women's Foundation for a Greater Memphis 1998

First Edition 1998
ISBN 0-9667740-0-0
Printed by Brunner Printing Co., Inc.
Memphis, Tennessee, USA

This book available from:
Women's Foundation for a Greater Memphis
$10.00 plus $4.50 shipping and handling

Cover by Kate Manzo
Interior design by Patrick Dugan

Dedicated to

Mertie Willigar Buckman

founder of the Women's Foundation for a Greater Memphis

whose vision and generosity continues to inspire others to give.

with grateful appreciation to

Peri Motamedi

a founding board member of the Women's Foundation

whose original suggestion led to the publication of this book.

WOMEN'S FOUNDATION
FOR A GREATER MEMPHIS

The Women's Foundation for a Greater Memphis is an inclusive alliance of women working together to promote philanthropy among women, foster women's leadership in the community, and advocate for and support programs, including those serving children, that enable women of all ages to reach their full potential.

ACKNOWLEDGMENTS

Special thanks to Mertie Buckman, for graciously and tirelessly answering seemingly endless rounds of questions, and to her family, especially her son, Bob Buckman, and his daughter, Kathy Davis. Nancy Cummins of Buckman Laboratories was a source of great knowledge and stacks of newspaper clippings, and Barbara McConville helped make interview arrangements and provided photographs. I am grateful to those who made time for personal interviews: Barbara Hyde, Ellen Rolfes, Gid Smith, Beth Dixon, Patricia Howard, Jim Daughdrill, Michael McGinniss, Patrick O'Brien, Dora Ivey, Tom Southard, Peri Motamedi, and Alma Pierotti. Appreciation also is extended to many persons who called or wrote to share stories of Mertie: Dr. P. K. Seidman, Beverly Nicholson, Gertrude Perdue, Kate Gooch, Jill Burkee, Lisa Bell, Loyd Templeton, Sherry Fields, Lorinne Cunningham, Eva Sladen, Marge Utterback, John Pera, J. Michael Krech, and Diane Goldstein. Last but not least, my appreciation to Jane Himes, whose earlier interviews with Mertie were transcribed and served as resources for the history of Buckman Laboratories.

Trish Calvert
Memphis, Tennessee

Contents

Prologue

A portrait, mounted in a large gilded frame, hangs in the foyer of Buckman Hall at Rhodes College in Memphis, Tennessee, in honor of the benefactress of the building. Mertie Willigar Buckman's white-haired likeness, with a modest smile shaping her lips, captures her open countenance and the direct gaze of her blue eyes. Few who pass through Buckman Hall fail to notice the portrait, although most do not know her apart from her legendary generosity. The students who carry backpacks slung carelessly over one shoulder as they hurry to classes are most likely unaware of her gifts that have made it possible for them to send frantic e-mails to professors whose thesis deadlines loom large. And this, perhaps, is as it was meant to be, for Mertie Buckman does not seek recognition, honor, or gratitude. Her generosity flows from a store of wealth and knowledge that, in her opinion, she was most fortunate to have acquired.

Wealthy benefactors or benefactresses often may be viewed as distant figures, but the monuments, buildings, and awards named in Mrs. Buckman's honor contradict this "distant" image. Wherever Mertie Buckman is honored, her active involvement in the institution's well being has permeated the place with her vibrant essence.

In Buckman Hall, on the grounds of Christian Brothers University, resides an impressive marble bas-relief sculpture depicting the spirit of harmony and generosity that Mertie Buckman brings to various aspects of the university community; the image of Mertie is the central figure, seated and holding flowers, and she is surrounded by representative figures for various components of education at CBU. The campus of St. Mary's Episcopal School includes the Mertie W. Buckman Performing and Fine Arts Center. The Raleigh location of the Young Women's Christian Association (YWCA) is named the Mertie Buckman Branch. With so much tangible evidence of Mertie Buckman's dedication to social and cultural improvement, it would be impossible not to be overawed and humbled by this community's First Lady of Philanthropy.

Upon meeting Mertie Buckman, one is struck by her forthright honesty, her modesty, and her egalitarian openness to friendships with diverse persons of wide-ranging backgrounds, regardless of status or influence. Although the walls of her office in the international headquarters of Buckman Laboratories in Memphis hold innumerable framed awards and certificates of appreciation, the awards are displayed only at the request of others; they have encouraged Mrs. Buckman to allow public knowledge of her philanthropy, as an example to others to do the same good work.

"We really had to convince her to let us do this [hang the awards], in preparation for the company's fiftieth anniversary celebration," explains Nancy Cummins, executive assistant to Mrs. Buckman. "It really isn't in her nature to put these on display," she says, as she waves her hand toward the award-decorated office walls.

Ms. Cummins, who assists Mrs. Buckman in scheduling appointments and conducting correspondence, offered assistance in gathering press clippings, transcripts, and photographs as the Women's Foundation For A Greater Memphis embarked upon compiling a book to honor Mertie's eventful life and significant civic contributions. Ms. Cummins knows the family well. "I wasn't used to being around wealthy people when I first came here," she confides. "The Buckmans are *real* people. Miss Mertie is very unassuming, quite down-to-earth. She's such a lovely person." Those sentiments would be echoed by community leaders who shared insights into the essence of Mertie Buckman.

"Mertie does not seek accolades or honors," confirms Brother Patrick O'Brien, director of major gifts and planned giving at Christian Brothers University. Her gift to construct Buckman Hall was not contingent upon its being named for her, and Brother Pat explains that she had to be convinced to concede to its being named in her honor. Tom Southard, headmaster of St. Mary's School, a college preparatory school for girls, agrees. "Mertie has come to understand that by making her philanthropic gifts and involvement public, rather than private, she encourages others in the community to do the same," he says, adding that "it is essential for our students to be presented with such a role model, a woman of influence who supports our work here financially. Mrs. Buckman is a pioneer in the support of education for girls and women."

Her reluctant concession to public recognition has, indeed, had an impact upon others' willingness to become involved and to contribute to Mertie's causes. When Mertie Buckman's name is associated with a project or campaign, the community listens and responds. She wields tremendous influence, in her soft-spoken but self-confident way. This influence results partially from her modesty and unassuming personal style and partially from her devoting herself only to causes that have personal meaning for her. Then, after thorough research and reaching the decision that a project is truly worthy, she follows the project with focused interest and attention to the details of good management.

"She's definitely a hands-on supporter," says Patricia Howard, executive director of Girls, Incorporated, an organization that targets education for girls around issues of concern to girls and women. "She asks very hard questions at committee meetings, and we're scrambling to keep up with her sometimes!"

One of Mertie's current projects is the Women's Foundation for a Greater Memphis, an organization which evolved from Mertie's gift of $50,000 to the Community Foundation of Greater Memphis in 1989, with the funds earmarked for supporting women's needs in the community. The mission of the Women's Foundation is simple, yet potentially profound: to promote philanthropy among women by establishing and nurturing an inclusive alliance of women throughout the community who advocate and support programs that benefit girls and women. The membership roster of the Women's Foundation Board of Directors attests to the influence of Mertie Buckman. The directors comprise a diverse alliance of women from many areas of interest and backgrounds, yet they successfully collaborate to create and maintain a network of beneficial support envisioned by Mertie for the Memphis community.

Although Mertie Buckman is the matriarch of a family that has contributed millions of dollars to the Memphis-area community, her legacy is that of a caring and generous spirit cherished by those who "knew her back when. . .," long before she was blessed with the wealth that is now well known. As a young woman of modest means, she participated in women's suffrage campaigns; as a young wife, she supported a graduate-student husband as a teacher of young women; as a young mother, she served in leadership positions in the local American Association of University Women. Mertie took an interest in local politics and championed the campaign to fluoridate city drinking water, offering a calm rationale— undoubtedly given weight due to her education and her dinner conversations with her chemist husband— for the necessary benefits of adding fluoride to the water. For the Church Women United she sold greeting cards to benefit the United Nations International Children's Education Fund (UNICEF), then later donned gardening gloves to plant flowers in the landscaping project for the Raleigh YWCA building that would one day bear her name. She also recruited friends and neighbors to serve as members of the newly formed Conference of Christians and Jews.

Even during the early years of her membership in Church Women United, she served with a hands-on, no-nonsense style of leadership. "I remember my first introduction to Mertie Buckman," recalls Gid Smith, now the president of the Community Foundation of Greater Memphis and then the director of the Metropolitan Interfaith Association (MIFA). "This was early on, but Mrs. Buckman already was known as a community leader. She was in her sixties, I imagine, and her organization, Church Women United, was operating on a shoestring budget. They had no office headquarters and had requested some space at MIFA, so they could store their papers and books." A bookcase for storage use had been ordered and sent to MIFA. Some time later, Mertie showed up at the MIFA office to drop off some CWU papers. "Well, that bookcase had not been assembled," says Gid Smith, "and it was just sitting in the hallway. So, Mertie came to me to request a screwdriver, ready to put the bookcase together herself." He chuckles as he remembers that "I was taken aback and hastened to help her, and together we got that bookcase put together." His anecdote illustrates the no-nonsense approach of Mertie Buckman, a self-reliant and competent woman ready to do whatever is necessary to complete a task.

It is her "giving of herself" or sense of responsibility that distinguishes the chronicle of Mertie Buckman's life. But just who *is* this woman of whom so many speak with affection and something akin to awe? Answers to that question, posed to those who know her—some who know her well and some who know her work—only begin to tell the story of Mertie. Hers is the story of a life well lived and of the myriad lives touched and influenced by the essence of Mertie.

Photograph Courtesy of Skipworth of Memphis

Friends

Those who speak of Mertie Buckman tell their own stories of who she is, what she is like, and how they have been touched by her influence. To some, she is reserved and dignified, but unerringly kind. To others, she is warm and approachable, or, in the words of Dora Ivey, a long-time companion and associate director of the YWCA, "a hoot." Some cite her fierce convictions, while others praise her calm and steady demeanor.

Men generally speak first of her quick mind and her attention to details of good management, while women usually speak first of affectionate regard and greeting her with an embrace or feeling inspired by her presence. All who know her commend her integrity and moral convictions, while members of her family offer admiring comments about her determination...a trait sometime described as "stubbornness." The picture that begins to emerge is that of a complex, multi-faceted, and highly regarded woman.

"She may let you get to know her, she may not...," warns her son, Robert Buckman, chairman of the board of directors of Bulab Holdings, at the beginning of this book project. "If you're lucky, you'll get a glimpse of a very, very complex woman. There are many layers there, many interests and experiences, and she is, in some ways, all things to all people. I will say this about Mother: she makes no distinctions in her friendships with people of different classes or backgrounds or status. She won't tolerate that."

His words shed light on observations made by friends of Mertie's. "I never want to waste her time," confides Gid Smith. "She likes to get down to business." And Dora Ivey has offered a subtle warning, "Mertie will not suffer fools." Comments from a long-time friend and colleague of the Buckman family, Dr. P. K. Seidman, convey warm admiration of Mrs. Buckman and another warning: "While much can be said [about Mertie] in 100 pages, [a profile] needs more to do justice to the person and the subject."

Her Work

Mertie Buckman cannot be known apart from her work. Invariably, any exploratory questions to her—inquiries into her feelings, thoughts, dreams, regrets—move full circle to her work. She shares her hopes for a particular organization and relates how associations and friendships were forged over planning meetings or during fundraising events. Ostensibly, whatever introspection occupies her mind occurs while her hands are actively engaged in the task of making lists, reviewing blueprints, or tallying numbers on a balance sheet. Since she has devoted her life to caring for a greater community, in a variety of small and large ways, her work tells the greater part of her story.

The roots of Mertie's philanthropic work go back to her early youth and the emphasis her family placed on concern for the wider community. Having been nurtured in an environment of civic awareness, Mertie's sense of social service developed naturally and grew stronger as she reached maturity. Once she and her husband, Dr. Stanley Buckman, were in the position to offer financial support to the broader community, they first targeted their alma maters, the University of Washington and the University of Minnesota. Then, over the years, they began to concentrate their philanthropic efforts in their adopted community of Memphis, which they consider home. "I think I've lived here long enough to be called a Memphian at heart," Mertie says with a smile.

This Memphian-at-heart became involved in volunteer work as a young wife and mother, rearing a family in Memphis while serving on the board of directors of Buckman Laboratories, the company she co-founded with her husband. Mertie devoted herself to a variety of causes: rallying volunteers to catalog books that were borrowed and solicited to establish the first public library in Raleigh, spreading the word about the American Cancer Society Cancer Crusade of 1964, serving on the board of managers of Church Women United, serving as the president of the board of directors of the YWCA, and serving on the boards of directors for Rhodes College and Christian Brothers University. Her association with many of the institutions she championed so many years ago continues today, in either an active or advisory role. She has not, however, closed her eyes to newer challenges. In 1989, she made a generous contribution to the Community Foundation of Greater Memphis for support of women's programs, which resulted in creation of the Women's Foundation for a Greater Memphis and of which Mertie serves as honorary chair. In September of 1997, she endowed Girls, Incorporated, of Memphis, with a gift of one million dollars.

Although Mertie's financial generosity is well known and greatly lauded, it is her personal attention and support that wins the hearts of those who work daily on the projects she funds. She has scrutinized blueprints for the Mertie Buckman Wing of the renovated Lucille Devore Tucker Center for Girls, Incorporated, and has pored over landscaping plans for the Christian Brothers University Buildings and Grounds Committee. "She's always asking questions, always with an eye for 'what can we do and for how much?'" says CBU's Brother Patrick O'Brien. "She gives money, and she gives her time," observes Beth Dixon, vice-president of development for the Community Foundation of Greater Memphis, who later became executive director of the Women's Foundation. "Although the Women's Foundation took some time to organize, Mertie never left her watch, always faithfully attending our planning sessions, offering suggestions, and following through with visits to women in the community to garner support."

Mertie's work is a testimonial to who she is, what is important to her, and what she wishes for the diverse community, with emphasis on girls and women, within the Memphis area.

Thrift and Generosity

"What I love about Mertie, and what very few people realize about her," says Dora Ivey, "is that her public acts of generosity are far, far eclipsed by her private acts of giving and caring." Off the record, Dora describes several instances of Mertie's quiet gifts of money, time, and caring offered without fanfare, often anonymously. Many times, the recipient is unaware that Mertie has made arrangements or contributed funds to benefit those truly in need. "And she doesn't want anyone to know," warns Dora. "She doesn't do it for recognition, but for others. She knows what it is like to have little, as well as to have much. She sees her wealth as a gift and passes it along. Besides, some people would be too proud to accept help."

A long-time fellow philanthropist and volunteer, Marge Utterback, concurs that Mertie has quietly supported many good causes with financial gifts through the years, without fanfare or recognition. Mrs. Utterback explains that Mertie agreed to attach her name to financial gifts only when she was persuaded that visibility was important in order to encourage other philanthropists to follow suit. "I remember a time," recalls Marge, "when women whose husbands were active in Boys Clubs wouldn't contribute to Girls Clubs because they felt that it was more important to contribute to boys, who one day would be heads of households. Mertie and I talked about this, and she agreed that it would be important to make our support of Girls Clubs [now Girls, Incorporated] more public." Marge also points out that Mertie always has been willing to support projects that met community needs, regardless of whether the projects were perceived as popular, prestigious, or "politically correct." One example is Mertie's having been a proponent of integrated meetings of local chapters of the American Association of University Women in the early 1960s, when other AAUW chapters across the country were at times bitterly divided over racial issues. Another example is Mertie's having championed a transitional center for women being released from prison at a time when public support for this project was low, recalls fellow Church Women United member Lorinne Cunningham. Mertie's volunteerism and

During Mertie's 90th birthday on October 19, 1994, at the Peabody Hotel in Memphis, her son, Robert H. Buckman was on hand to congratulate his mother.
(Photograph from personal collection of Mertie Buckman)

Above: *Among those celebrating Mertie's 80th birthday were Bessie Mayer (left) and Delcinia Dickens (right).*
Photograph from personal collection of Mertie Buckman.

Granddaughter Kathy Buckman Davis (left) joined her father, Robert Buckman, and Melba Schmitz (right) to celebrate Mertie's 80th birthday on October 19, 1984.
Photograph from personal collection of Mertie Buckman.

Also on hand to celebrate Mertie's 80th birthday were long-time friends (left to right) Jane Himes, Melba Schmitz (in front), Bill Stitt, first marketing person for Buckman Laboratories in 1945, and Marjorie Stitt.
Photograph from personal collection of Mertie Buckman.

Right: *Marjorie Stitt, a friend of Mertie's since 1945, traveled from Anacortes, Washington to join the 80th birthday celebration.*
Photograph from personal collection of Mertie Buckman.

financial gifts are tangible expressions of her personal convictions, and her living by her convictions serves as an inspiration to others to support meaningful projects.

Mertie Buckman is matter-of-fact, but never casual, about money. She is quite aware of the value of a dollar. As a woman whose early adult years were engulfed by the Great Depression, she displays the daily frugality characteristic of her generation. "She saves everything, recycles aluminum foil, and scoops out the inside of eggs to get the last drop when she's baking," observes her granddaughter, Kathy Davis, as she describes Mertie's putting her principles into practice. Mertie reared her children and grandchildren to work hard, save money, and set goals. "The summer I was 16, I told Grandmother I was working to save money for a sewing machine. She liked that, since it was a practical goal and one that was dear to her heart...she was interested in sewing and textiles," Kathy recalls. "When I had saved up about half the needed money, she made up the rest and bought me the sewing machine. I wasn't expecting that, and I was so excited!"

Mertie's life-long thriftiness is well known by her family and friends, as Brother Patrick O'Brien attests. "We traveled together to Italy to visit Jill Burkee, the artist who sculpted *The Essence of Mertie* for the college," he says, referring to the marble sculpture honoring Mertie on the Christian Brothers University campus. "We toured Europe extensively, visiting museums and stopping for meals, and Mertie was in charge of accounting for expenses. I would often round off amounts and occasionally make up the difference out of my pocket when it was time to pay a bill, but she would have none of that," he recalls, with a smile of obvious

For Mertie's 90th birthday on October 19, 1994, four generations of the Buckman family gathered at the historic Peabody Hotel in Memphis to celebrate her entry into nonagenarian status.
Photograph from personal collection of Mertie Buckman.

admiration. "She was exact down to the penny."

Brother Pat feels that Mertie is frugal in order to be generous. She is reluctant to spend money on herself, because she doesn't feel the need, but she is never hesitant to give meaningful gifts that produce an impact. If the need arises, she is spontaneously generous. Brother Pat continues to reflect upon their travels in Italy and describes an incident during their visit to the Vatican for an audience with the Pope. Sitting near them on the pew was an Irishwoman who was in difficult circumstances, and, after hearing her story, Mertie asked Brother Pat to quietly pass on a hundred-dollar bill to the woman. Mertie was touched by the woman's story and was quick to respond with assistance.

Brother Pat also shares a photograph of himself and Mertie, taken during her 90th birthday party, and points to her red dress in the photo. "She bought a new dress for the party," he chuckles, "and that was unusual for Mertie, so the birthday celebration was a special one."

Her son, Robert Buckman, also chuckles over Mertie's frugality. "Is she frugal?! It's downright ridiculous at times. She won't spend a penny on herself unless she's convinced it's absolutely necessary," he observes. Although it took some time, Bob finally convinced his mother to trade in her old car for a safer, larger Mercedes.

"But she won't let me hire a driver; nor will she allow anyone to live with her, although she needs some help at times. She says it's a waste of money, and she doesn't want someone sitting around in the car waiting for her while she's shopping or waiting at the doctor's office…or whatever. She won't even let me pay for it." His vexed expression conveys his frustration, albeit affectionate, with his mother's frugality and strong independence.

Mertie Buckman with
Brother Patrick O'Brien
Photo courtesy of CBU, Memphis.

Independence

Mertie's personal sense of independence is widely known and admired, and her self-sufficiency is regarded as even more remarkable as she ages, since she has the financial means to employ persons for assistance. Yet she rarely does so, preferring to do for others and avoid being an imposition. Even now, in her nineties, Mertie looks for ways to be of assistance, pursuing a helping role that is of central importance to her.

"This past summer, I went to see *Casablanca* at the Orpheum as Mertie's guest. She also invited her grandchildren, Kathy and Karl," Dora Ivey relates, "and Mertie drove carpool, of course!" The evening of their outing, the motorized traffic was heavy and there was a Harley-Davidson convention in Memphis, with motorcyclists roaring past the car at high speeds. Mertie negotiated the traffic without missing a beat, pulled up to the theater, and announced to the three adults who were her passengers: "All right, now you all get out, and I'll go park the car." Dora shakes her head, with a bemused expression reflecting both admiration and frustration. "No, Mertie," she responded. "You get out, and we'll park the car." Being "waited upon" is a selfish trait never cultivated by Mertie Buckman.

Tales abound of Mertie's independence and stamina, and friends tell those tales with abashed respect for this woman who reminds us that our preconceptions about what life should be in the later years are false and, perhaps, even offensive. Eva Sladen, whose husband Brian joined Buckman Laboratories in 1963, remembers long treks with Mertie through England and South Africa. They shared walks through the countryside, encounters with hippos on a game reserve, horseback rides, and long hikes in the Drakensberg, South Africa. "Mertie, twenty-six years my senior, would walk me off my feet!" she exclaims.

Dr. James Daughdrill, president of Rhodes College, recalls attending a Buckman Laboratories board of directors' meeting in Brazil in the late 1980s, along with Mertie. "My wife, Libby, and I privately wondered about Mertie's strength, about whether she would be able to keep up with the group as we changed planes and managed the hassles of luggage and customs," Jim admits. However, Mertie, then in her late eighties, handled her own luggage at the airport and walked faster than anyone; the Daughdrills had trouble keeping up with her. "I remember saying to Libby, 'This is the damnedest thing...I don't believe this!'" as they scurried to match Mertie's pace.

Now into her ninth decade, Mertie continues to pursue her interests, pleasures, and commitments. Her pastor, the Reverend J. Michael Krech of Raleigh Presbyterian Church, counts Mertie among the faithful in attendance virtually every Sunday. He recalls her trekking through snow and ice one January Sunday that had kept most of the considerably younger members of the congregation at home. Her faithfulness and sense of responsibility are what have "made her so dear to so many for so long," says the Reverend Krech. Mertie's church involvement includes not only faithful attendance and financial support but also participation in a recent stage production at the church. Her friend Eva Sladen describes Mertie's thespian contribution as delightful. "She put on a splendid performance and her improvisations for the lines that eluded her were better than the original script…she got a standing ovation!"

There is a core of strength in Mertie that defies her age. "She's tough as a Texas boot-heel," says Jim Daughdrill, quickly qualifying her toughness as being equally matched by her tender heart. Her contributions to board meetings, both at Rhodes College and at Buckman Laboratories, are focused, to-the-point, and insightful. "She'll occasionally point out some detail that's been overlooked or some obstacle that needs to be addressed. She comes out with a 'zinger' every once in a while that keeps us on our toes," he continues, with open admiration. "She asks the most penetrating questions and cuts right to the heart of the matter."

Colleagues at Girls, Incorporated, the YWCA, CBU, and the Community Foundation concur with Jim Daughdrill. "Mertie follows the balance sheet very carefully, and I don't feel too confident when I see her adding up the numbers," says Brother Michael McGinniss, CBU president. Mertie asks tough questions, keeps organizations focused on their missions, and sums up issues in insightful quips that provide a point of focus and the relief of good humor.

Children

Although Mertie Buckman is known for her commitment to education and her advocacy and love for children, it is less well known that children, in return, seem to flock to her. Her innate affection for children is reflected in her ability to see their potential, to share their spirit of exuberance, and to accept their naiveté from the perspective of having lived life much longer than they may be able to imagine. Mertie's delight in children is obvious as she speaks of her own great-grandchildren, commenting on their unique personalities and her appreciation of their differences. She is inherently empathetic, identifying with the perspectives of her twin six-year-old great-grandchildren, whom she recently visited in New Mexico. "One is quite extroverted, one is a little more shy. I think he needs a little encouragement," she muses aloud, perhaps making a mental note to send him a new addition to his growing rock collection. It is rare for children to be blessed by the interest of an adult who is able to see the world projected through the eyes of a child. "Children will go their own way, they will live their own lives, but they will need encouragement and plenty of education," Mertie says, offering a glimpse of her own style of mothering. Mertie's face softens as she speaks of the needs of children, those in her family and those in the community.

"Mertie is dedicated to the children we serve," says Patricia Howard of Girls, Incorporated, an organization that offers child care and educational programs primarily directed to girls living in low income areas of the community. "She is appreciative of any token of gratitude from our girls and wants to meet them personally. She receives poems and notes from the girls, then searches out the girls when she visits our centers. She likes to get to know the kids, and I've seen her walk through a crowd of adults just to get to the children."

Children who are fortunate enough to know Mertie Buckman speak of her with a mixture of awe and affection. "Students at St. Mary's are drawn to her, whether they are of kindergarten age or seniors in the twelfth grade," says Tom Southard, headmaster of Memphis' St. Mary's Episcopal School for Girls. "Many times I have seen students come up to her, touch her, ask her questions. Their love for her is so natural and so genuine. Her warmth and goodness are like magnets to children."

Mertie is well known to and well loved by the girls of St. Mary's, who have long associated her name with improvements to the school. The recently constructed Mertie W. Buckman Performing and Fine Arts Center is casually referred to on campus as "The Mert," and the girls' affection for Mrs. Buckman is as uncontrived as the nickname for her building. St. Mary's parent, Beth Dixon, then vice-president of development for Community Foundation of Greater Memphis and later named executive director of the Women's Foundation for a Greater Memphis, shares the story of her daughter Ellis' first encounter with Mertie Buckman. Ellis had transferred to St. Mary's in the sixth grade and knew nothing of Mertie Buckman. About four years ago, the school celebrated Mertie Buckman Day, and Mrs. Buckman was the honored guest for lunch. Ellis came home that day to tell her mother all about "this lady named Mertie Buckman,

who has her own money, lots of it, and has given a lot to the school." But what was most impressive to Ellis, and what Beth values most, was that Mertie joined in the celebration as a participant. She did not offer a prepared speech during the occasion, but instead shared lunch with the students, visited at their tables, and joined in the banter of young girls. "And, Mom, she would let people come up to her and give her hugs," Ellis related excitedly. "She let us *touch* her." Beth smiles as she relates the story, adding that it is a poignant example of Mertie as a role model to so many young girls—teaching by example as she gives of herself from a wealth of independence and financial blessings. "We have such a need for women to demonstrate this type of generosity and caring in our community," Beth says, "for the benefit of generations to come."

Tom Southard agrees. He hopes Mertie is aware of the impact she has had on so many through her presence and generosity, and that she serves as a role model for young and old, male and female, in the Memphis community. "Every girl at St. Mary's will be reminded daily of the potential in her life, not only in terms of what can be accomplished by a woman, but also how one's life can be shared for the benefit of all," he says. "I recently heard a younger St. Mary's girl say, 'I want to grow up and be like Mertie Buckman, so I can do things like she does for others.'"

Loving Life

Mertie Buckman's vibrancy endures in her presently attained age of 93. She continues to read extensively, saving newspaper clippings and magazine articles to share items of interest with friends and colleagues. "She probably gets more mail than I do," says Brother Michael McGinniss, president of CBU, "and she reads it!" She is a nature lover and an avid gardener, whose living room abounds with houseplants and African violets. "She loves wildflowers," says her son Bob, relating her ongoing battle with the gardeners who often fail to leave her wildflowers intact as they weed and prune. She also tours art shows and antiques museums with attention to minute detail. "I'm astounded by how long she looks at things," says Brother Pat, recalling his museum trips with Mertie through France and Italy. When she gives in to her need for rest, the respite is of brief duration. "At one point in our journeys, we took a side trip to Chartres, and she wanted to push on to visit a museum. Instead of heading for the hotel for an afternoon of rest, we sat on a park bench for a while, for a little nap, and then on we went," he recalls.

Her myriad interests and activities keep her quite busy, and her busy life is reflected in a heavily scheduled appointment book. Although she prefers to sleep until she awakens naturally, she will rise early to attend the 7:30 a.m. board meetings at CBU; she arrives alert, with notes in hand and questions in mind. Her many social and business engagements include regularly visiting her office at Buckman Laboratories, dining out at a favorite restaurant—Paulette's in mid-town—and using her season tickets for plays and musicals. She has a standing Wednesday appointment at her hair dresser's, and she continues to plan out-of-town trips.

Tom Southard is familiar with Mertie's love of travel and new experiences. "On our trip to South Carolina on school business, we attended Camden Cup, a steeplechase event. Most of the day, there was a constant drizzle of rain, with wind and cloudiness. I was especially worried about Mrs. Buckman, but while many of us were concerned with staying dry, rather than watching the races, Mrs. Buckman, in her rainhat and raincoat, with a small umbrella, never veered from the day's objective of enjoying the races."

Other friends and colleagues tell tales of Mertie's making the most of unfortunate circumstances and of enjoying experiences as they come. Gertrude Purdue, a long-time friend and associate in Church Women United, recalls a CWU Retreat she attended with Mertie, and the retreat was marred by very bad weather. "To this day, we joke and laugh about the experience we had three decades ago at Lakeshores Conference Grounds. The temperature dropped suddenly, and we were totally unprepared. In a dormitory, some half-a-dozen women gathered sweaters, throw rugs, and anything else that would keep us warm. Mertie and I huddled together, and I tell her to this very day that she saved me from freezing to death!" The lingering memories among her friends of experiences shared with Mertie revolve around tolerant good humor and her ability to "make the best of it" when plans go awry.

"Mertie is a true participant, and she obviously enjoys being a part of the action," observes Kate Gooch, president of the Memphis Arts Council. Kate recalls a ballet performance presented at the Memphis Botanical Garden, co-sponsored by the Arts Council's Art in the Schools Program and the University of Memphis Department of Dance. "It was a participatory ballet, and the audience of school children moved from scene to scene, set in the different gardens. Mertie went along with us through the Garden, keeping up with the children and laughing along with them when the dancers asked the children to make fish sounds! It was a wonderful and memorable experience to watch her enjoyment of the dance and of the children." Kate speaks of Mertie's love of the arts and her advocacy for children, emphasizing Mrs. Buckman's continuing support of the Arts Council's mission to bring the arts into the everyday experience of children. "She is a great supporter and a woman of profound influence. We are truly indebted to her."

Connection

Although Mertie Buckman's good works and gifts are resoundingly admired and appreciated, it is her personal presence or magnetism that distinguishes her. She possesses the unique qualities of integrity and wholeness—a strong sense of self—that speaks to those who seek comfort and inspiration from her presence. Persons of all ages and all walks of life are drawn to Mertie, responding to who she is and not to what she has materially.

Maxine Smith, former executive secretary of the Memphis Chapter of the National Association for the Advancement of Colored People (NAACP) and a board member of the Women's Foundation for a Greater Memphis, spoke at a Women's Foundation reception in September of 1997 to honor Mertie and to announce the Foundation's Mertie Buckman Mentor Awards. These awards, presented to women who have served as mentors to other women, were initiated to recognize those influenced by and following the example of Mertie's daily giving of herself to others. At the reception, Maxine reads a long list of Mertie Buckman's accomplishments and awards, including her being the recipient of the 1996 Community Service Award from the Memphis Rotary Club, the 1993 Humanitarian of the Year Award from the National Conference of Christians and Jews, the 1992 Outstanding Citizen of the Year Award from the Memphis Civitan Clubs, and being named in 1991 as the Person of Vision by the Alliance for the Blind and Visually Impaired.

Enhancing the tribute for the twenty-five honorees gathered in the room is Maxine's departure from her prepared speech: She looks up from her notes to gaze directly at Mertie and says simply, "We love you,

Mertie." Maxine continues her extemporaneous comments by relating her personal story of Mertie's compassion and kindness to her. She speaks tearfully of her "blessed mother," who led an active and productive life until her recent death in her late nineties, and how Mertie's own productive life reminds her of her mother's hard work and good example. She also speaks of how Mertie's influence led to her involvement at the Women's Foundation and to include the crusade for women in her life's work of crusading against racism. Maxine's voice is powerfully mesmerizing as she addresses the assembled audience of women from many walks of life and diverse backgrounds.

Following the conclusion of the formal program, Maxine Smith continues to reflect upon Mertie's essence. "I don't know what it is about Mertie," she says, shaking her head, "but she is a powerful woman." And that power is no less potent because it is subtle and wielded softly, with feminine grace. Maxine sees in Mertie the strength of character possessed by her own mother and is comforted by this sense of connection.

Many others share this sense of connection with Mertie, because she is attuned to those around her and directs her energy toward others. Her empathy quietly shines beneath her calm demeanor. "She is a truly calm woman able to see things sensibly, able to smooth over problems," says Peri Motamedi, a Persian-American artist who serves with Mertie on the Women's Foundation board of directors. "When I am distressed, when things are not going well, I will speak to her, and she sees things well. This is part of my culture, to honor the older woman and to appreciate her perspective, which is long. It is a help." Peri sees in

Mertie the calm assurance of a woman who has lived a longer life and acquired experience and wisdom, and it is from Mertie's tempered strength that she draws reinforcement and sense of purpose.

"Mertie is full of fun and laughter," says Dora Ivey. "She laughs like a kid at times and is a breath of fresh air. I never leave her without saying, 'I love you,' and I really do."

"She's such a warm person. I'd be offended if she didn't hug me when I see her," says Patricia Howard.

"Mertie has beauty, flexiblity, and a gift for becoming part of a group for the sheer enjoyment of it," observes Barbara Hyde, immediate past chair of the Women's Foundation.

"I remember Mertie from my early days at the company," says Dr. John Pera, a former director of Buckman Laboratories. "Dr. Buckman was a demanding man to work for, but such a remarkable man. Mertie was the heart of the company, and we all shared tremendous fondness for her. She is a friend to all and has connections with people all over the world who would call her a friend."

This widespread sense of friendship, of connection, is the common thread among those who attempt to describe Mertie's appeal, her essence. True to her selfless nature, Mertie eschews praise for her personal magnetism and focuses attention on her work and the value of philanthropy in building community. "I don't think we should idealize people," she states. "It is important for others to see the work, to follow in giving, and to support one another. Women, in particular, need to work together to help one another."

Mertie's humility and selflessness, combined with her commitment to serving humanity, strike receptive chords in her friends and acquaintances. Although Mertie has a wide circle of friends who share her goals, it is likely that few know her inner essence. She remains a very private, self-contained individual. A very real part of Mertie's gift in connecting with fellow human beings is her ability to nurture the belief that they do, indeed, know her; that their connection is mutually beneficial; and that their interaction offers the opportunity for personal growth. The psychological term for this personal empathy is transference: seeing in others that which we need or want to see, that which is perhaps lacking in ourselves. Mertie has an uncanny ability to connect with persons on this level and to offer just what they need at the time to contribute more fully to their work, their lives, and their families.

This personal connection or bonding is without artifice or contrivance for, above all else, Mertie is authentic and never phony. Secure within herself, her approach is straight-forward and sincere as she encourages others to recognize their full potential as unique human beings. Her talent in this area was recognized quickly by Brother Michael McGinniss, a relative newcomer to the Memphis community. In the three years he has served as president of Christian Brothers University, he has associated many times with Mrs. Buckman. "When I think of Mertie, I am reminded of a small pamphlet that circulated within our academic circle a few years ago: *On Confirming the Deepest Thing in Another*. It was written by Douglas Steere, who has worked extensively with the Christian Brothers in their mission of Christian education." The small booklet contains fascinating theories on the qualities requisite in good teachers. Steere records a

conversation with philosopher Martin Buber, who wrote of the power of meaningful connection between two individuals when they come together and share their deepest selves. Buber discusses the power of this interpersonal connection, as well as the importance of confirming what is real and meaningful in the soul or essence of the other person. It is easy to understand why Brother Michael associates Mertie with this philosophical precept, for she personifies the principle in her rare ability to confirm what is real and worthy is those she meets.

Humor

Because her friends speak of Mertie Buckman with ready smiles and spontaneous amusement as they recall their experiences with her, it is obvious that Mertie's presence is imbued with good humor. It is a subtle sense of humor, however, consisting of a twinkle in her eye and an unexpected wry or witty comment, rather than a propensity for telling jokes. "Mertie likes to participate in the banter and friendly teasing that is a part of our gathering together to begin board meetings, and she enjoys a good story. She has a finely developed sense of humor," says Brother McGinniss of his association with Mertie at Christian Brothers University. She readily joins in the casual exchange among groups of colleagues, and she seems to enjoy the good-natured teasing that seems inevitable when her family gathers. Her down-to-earth humor shines through her calm demeanor with quicksilver speed and often belies her sensible, business-like attitude—revealing an unerring sense of tongue-in-cheek understatement to her friends and associates.

Ellen Rolfes, then director of the Women's Foundation, is quick to point out Mertie's quiet humor and playful side. Ellen describes Mertie with frank admiration, saying, "Mertie has an open spirit, so she joins in with a playful, exuberant group as easily as she commands attention in a boardroom of people in somber business suits." Mertie took part in a recent retreat for members of the board of directors of the Women's Foundation. "This was an opportunity for our very diverse board to welcome each other's differences and build a community spirit for celebrating the cause of women's education. One of our board members, poet Marilou Awiakta, led us in a dance of celebration to honor our founder, and Mertie was given the place of honor in the center of the circle of dancers. But Mertie soon joined us in dancing, saying, 'No, this time I will dance!' And she did!" Mertie also recalls the retreat's events. Her eyes light up as she speaks of Marilou's unique, many-layered personality and of her ability to inspire others by sharing her Cherokee heritage and teachings. Mertie's delight in the gifts of various cultures is obvious.

Brother Pat chuckles as he recalls Mertie's enjoyment of dancing. During their 1993 trip to Italy, he and Mertie were invited one evening to join sculptress Jill Burkee's family at a restaurant in a traditional working-class community. The evening included music and dancing, and Mertie greatly enjoyed joining in the dancing. "And she danced with a communist that night!" Brother Pat laughs, obviously enjoying the telling of an often-repeated story. "Of course, in this part of Italy," he adds, "the overwhelming majority of working-class people had registered with the Communist Party early in their economic struggles."

Tom Southard remarks on Mertie's quick wit as he recalls a frantic "white-knuckle" trip to the airport, with Mrs. Buckman as a passenger and St. Mary's director of development at the wheel as the automobile sped down Interstate 240 to meet a scheduled flight. They made the connection, finished their business in South Carolina, and enjoyed a more leisurely drive from the airport upon their return to Memphis. This time Tom Southard was behind the wheel, driving at the posted speed limit, and the conversation turned to how slowly traffic was moving. At that point, Mrs. Buckman turned to the director of development, seated in the back, and commented, "You really enjoy a speedier approach, don't you?" All passengers in the automobile broke out in laughter, remembering their earlier race through Memphis in a breath-taking action scenario apropos to *The French Connection*.

Mertie's down-to-earth roots often are revealed in her impromptu remarks. One example of this earthy wit occurred when Mertie accompanied Brother Pat as he prepared for a university function. Among his tasks, he picked up an order previously placed for wine and liquor to serve as refreshments for the event. Upon their return to the university, Mertie quipped to Brother Pat's colleague that they had been on a "rum run" to get liquor.

Last summer, Mertie attended a performance of "*STOMP!*" at the Orpheum. "This was a rousing musical, with lots of loud music and an insistent beat to the music," recalls Dora Ivey. "I looked over at her about midway through the show and thought she had dozed off, although I couldn't be sure. When I shifted toward her, she opened one eye and said, 'I'm just feeling the beat!'"

During the course of interviews for this biography, Mertie is informed that her friends speak admiringly of her and are eager to furnish examples of her accomplishments, her wit, and her independence. In response, she chuckles with amusement, "Well, I imagine they're just amazed that a body as old as this just keeps going!"

In Mertie's case, mind rules matter. The essential elements of her essence—her indomitable spirit and courage, her openness to discovery and new interactions, and her commitment to leaving her world a better place than she found—combine to fuel her life force. This quintessential nonagenarian does, indeed, just keep going…spiritually impervious to time's passage since her physical form entered the world in 1904.

Flora Mertie Willigar, age 6, with her treasured teddy bear and doll near the Willigar family home in Lyme, New Hampshire, in 1910.
Photograph from personal collection of Mertie Buckman.

Heritage

Mertie's New England heritage forms the immutable core of her essence, and she readily speaks of her stoic, frontier-taming ancestors over the past 300 years. With an underlying trace of family pride, she cradles a small 14-inch statue in her hands and reads the inscription, "Hannah Dustin, Granite State Heroine of 1697." Although the sculptor romanticized the female figure by clothing her in an off-the-shoulder gown, the tomahawk and scalp she holds in her hands are authentic elements of Hannah Dustin's colonial New Hampshire story. And Mertie enjoys describing the courage and fortitude of her foremothers in both New Hampshire and Massachusetts.

Hannah Dustin was abducted from Haverhill, Massachusetts, in

1697 by a band of Indians following the birth of her thirteenth child. ("Women were strong and had lots of children in those days," Mertie wryly observes.) The woman who was nursing the new mother and infant also was abducted, and the captives, along with a young English boy, were taken to the Indians' riverside camp. After some time, the captives realized that their captors were planning to sell them into slavery. As they urgently planned their escape, attempts were made to ferret out information on the warriors' battle techniques. One of them probably inquired of an unsuspecting warrior, "When you attack, what do you do to knock out your enemy in one blow?" Taking the bait, the skilled warrior demonstrated his prowess, thus educating the captives to the technique that would be used to subdue them when they attempted to escape. When a propitious time arrived for flight, Hannah and the other captives attacked their male captors and fled the camp to escape in one of the war-

Mertie Willigar during a rowboat outing in New Hampshire, summer of 1919.
Photograph from personal collection of Metie Buckman.

riors' canoes, chopping holes in the remaining canoes so that they couldn't be pursued by water. According to the account, the liberated captives feared their story might not be believed, so they returned to the camp and scalped the men they had killed. After Hannah

was reunited with her husband, Thomas Dustin, he claimed the legal bounty for his wife's gruesome patches of warriors' hair.

In both New Hampshire and Massachusetts stand statues honoring Hannah Dustin's colonial valor. "She was the first woman in the United States to have a statue erected in her honor," Mertie says softly, studying the small replica of the large New Hampshire statue. Her thoughtful face reflects her appreciation for her New England heritage of stoicism in adversity, of practicality and frugality in daily living, and of modesty and reticence in relating courageous feats.

New Englander Flora Mertie Willigar was born on October 19, 1904, in Lyme, New Hampshire, a small farming community 10 miles north of Hanover. Her mother, Hattie Della Dustin Willigar, was a native of New Hampshire, and her father, Stephen Albert Willigar, was a transplanted Nova Scotian. Together they reared their family on a small dairy farm in Lyme. Mertie, named for a close friend of her mother's, was nurtured by her parents to possess a strong work ethic and a sense of responsibility for family. Her feeling of familial responsiblity was intensified when her mother died during Mertie's thirteenth year. Mertie describes her youth as one of "satisfaction derived from hard work" on the farm. "The women in the household were in charge of the chickens," she recalls, and her chores included operating the "horse rake," a piece of horse-drawn equipment that pulled hay into rolls for drying.

Mertie received her early education in a two-room schoolhouse in Lyme, where she completed the eighth grade. Following elementary school, her parents sent her to a nearby boarding school. She describes her first experience at the school as "rough," since the school was newly established and rather disorganized; the students were unsupervised in the dormitories and responsible for preparing their own fires and food. "My mother thought it was a bit much for me at such a young age, so I returned home after a week and spent another year in grade school," she recalls. To assist the young student, her teacher supplemented her classwork to match Mertie's abilities. The following year, Mertie again embarked upon a secondary-school education, being enrolled in an established Methodist boarding school, the Tilton School, in Tilton, New Hampshire.

During those years, Mertie's life-long commitment to the importance of education for females was forged, prompted by her own family history of hard-won educational opportunities for girls. She had first-hand knowledge of her grandfather's belief that his son, rather than his daughter, should be the beneficiary of any "extra" in the family's limited income and be given the opportunity to pursue higher education. Her ire is obvious as she com-

In 1919, two years after her mother's death, Mertie Willigar (left), age 15, and her younger sister, Bernis Willigar, were photographed with their horse and pony, respectively, near the family home in Lyme, New Hampshire.
Photograph from personal collection of Mertie Buckman.

ments with scornful disbelief, "And he wasn't the least bit interested in going on to school!" Since the family budget could be stretched only for this son's education, Mertie's grandmother sent her daughter to live with relatives to obtain formal schooling. Thus, Mertie's memory of her mother's frustration and disappointment in the societal belief that girls were not entitled to opportunities "inherent" for males shaped her fierce determination in her later philanthropic pursuits to "help shape an even playing field" for education of girls and women.

Mertie muses at length as she reminisces about her mother. "One thing I'll never forget is a lesson Mama taught me in my early years…when I probably was a pre-schooler," she recalls. Her mother sent her into town to the post office with two cents for a stamp and an envelope. Young Mertie happened to see the town physician slip a piece of mail into the mail slot, and she decided she could do the same—without purchasing a stamp. This she did, then spent her mother's two cents on candy, which was promptly consumed. By the time she returned home, the postmistress had called her mother to convey the news of the young girl's transgression. "I was so *embarrassed* to have to go back there and apologize," she confesses, but the incident provided an indelible lesson in honesty that remains with her to this day, almost nine decades later.

Another indelible impression in Mertie's memory is the woman described as having had the greatest influence, aside from her mother, in her life. "She was my third-grade teacher in 1912. She was a widow, who worked to support her two boys." Despite the fact that life was extremely difficult for her and her sons, she excelled in her teaching position. "She was very good, strict, and precise in her lessons," Mertie recalls, nodding in approval. She recalls another influential teacher, Miss Emerson, who also was very strict, but "I just loved her." Away from the classroom, Miss Emerson was warm and sharing; she would rent a cottage in the summers and take her students there for outings of swimming in the lake or climbing mountains. These early experiences and their impact upon her are recalled fondly.

Also fondly recalled is Mertie's growing up in a small community where neighbors looked out for one another, an environment especially supportive at a time in America when rapid and precedent-setting changes were taking place. Changes in the forms of transportation created lasting milestones in her memory, and she evokes childhood memories of having traveled by horse and buggy or by sleigh during winter months. When she was six years old, she experienced her first ride in an automobile. "They were improving the state road between Lyme and Hanover, and some of the men who were working on the road had automobiles." She convinced one of the workers to give her a ride in his new machine, which resulted in another unforgettable "first" for her. "It was fun!" she says, with a girlish grin. She also vividly recalls her first airplane flight in the early 1930s from Minneapolis to Chicago. "It was on the same type of 'plane that [Charles] Lindbergh flew" when he made the world's first solo nonstop transatlantic flight in 1927. During her own first flight, she was too excited by the new adventure to be fearful or nervous. "The day was cloudy and very windy, so I *did* experience some motion sickness and was a little sick to my stomach," she laughs. The slight physical discomfort was, however, totally eclipsed by the excitement of her new experience.

Ever open to progressive domestic developments, Mertie joined her mother in following news of the women's suffrage movement leading to the successful ratification of the Nineteenth Amendment in 1920. "We were all for it," she declares, recalling public marches during the campaign and a youthful awareness that the votes-for-women movement was a ground-breaking effort that unified thousands upon thousands of women from diverse socio-economic backgrounds. "At that time in our town, women were allowed *only* to elect members and serve on the school board," so both she and her mother were strong advocates for women obtaining equal participation in civic activities. "Mama had a certain independence that was remarkable for her time," she says, with obvious admiration. Mertie's mother was an early "woman of independent means," since she had inherited her parents' farm when the estate was settled after the senior Dustins' deaths. "My father purchased the farm from my mother when they married," she explains. "So my mother had her own money, her own property, and a certain standing in the community. She kept her money separate from his, and I went to college on her money."

Mertie digresses from her autobiographical odyssey to elaborate upon her belief that any woman's having a separate source of income is a valuable asset. Being financially independent is essential for women to establish a sense of self-sufficiency and to provide the opportunity, if needed, for women to escape difficult circumstances. She speaks of the plight of battered women and of their financial, as well as emotional, dependence upon men. When men "control the purse," she observes, women are especially vulnerable to being victimized.

Resuming the chronicle of her youth, Mertie relates that after she completed secondary school, she returned to the farm to help her father and her younger sister, Bernis. Since her mother had died of cancer after her first year at the Tilton School, she was needed at home to assist with chores and housekeeping. She had a vague longing to continue her education, but she was unsure which direction to follow. When her father asked her, "Well, what courses would you take if you went to college?", she couldn't answer his question. So, she remained at home on the farm and tended to her father and sister, while performing necessary domestic chores such as canning, making jelly, and cooking meals for the seasonal workers at the farm during hay-harvesting season. "It was hard, hard work," she remembers, and it was more difficult for her because she had little experience in bearing the full responsiblity of managing a busy farm.

She "kept house" for three years and took a position teaching at the primary school in Lyme, where she had first learned to read. She taught grades one through four and recalls feeling inadequate for the task; she realized that she did not want to continue indefinitely as a teacher. Nor did she want to continue indefinitely as the poorly prepared manager of the family farm—a laborious job which overwhelmed her—so she reached the conclusion that education in home economics was sorely needed and that would be her course of study in college.

Unexpectedly, her plans veered sharply. When Mertie was 19, her father died suddenly. "He had been unhappy in his last years," she says simply, explaining that he had continued to mourn for her deceased mother. "Men are more vulnerable to loss than women. They are wrapped up in their work and have fewer relationships; when those relationships are gone, they are at a loss," she muses reflectively. "They only pretend to be self-sufficient."

Mertie was thrust into the role of head of the family unit. After her father's death, she and her sister had no relatives living in New England. An uncle, who resided in Washington State, sent word for her and Bernis to join his family there. Bernis had been planning to attend boarding school that fall, and Mertie saw no need to uproot her sister, so she sent a telegram to her aunt and uncle, explaining that she and her sister would join them as soon as Bernis had finished her year of secondary school. Thus Mertie, at age 20, supervised her sister's education and prepared to bid farewell to a young man with whom she had been keeping company. "His name was Jack Pushee," she says, and she was fond of him. He was kind and helpful, later accompanying her and Bernis as far as Montreal on their train trip to Washington State. "It was difficult [to sever ties with her beau], but it was time to move on…it had to be done. We [later] corresponded for some time."

In keeping with her New England heritage of stoic pragmatism, Mertie held an auction to sell the farm and equipment, horse, buggy, sleigh, and automobile. Then she and her sister embarked upon their journey by rail to the Pacific Northwest, leaving their roots in New Hampshire. "It was time to go," she says softly.

Their aunt met the young women in Vancouver, then they traveled on to Puyallup, Washington. There, Bernis enrolled in high school, and Mertie enrolled in the nearby University of Washington. She later received a bachelor's and a master's degree in home economics, specializing in textiles. One of her school friends participated in a program to study abroad, and Mertie thought, "Well, if she can do it, then so can I." She applied to the program and spent a summer studying in Europe. "It was a wonderful experience," says Mertie. "I just loved it, learning and traveling to new places." (She would later relate some of her undergraduate and graduate experiences to Brother Patrick O'Brien, director of development for Christian Brothers University, leading him to comment that Mertie "has experienced a rather bohemian lifestyle, studying on the west coast in a time when women were a novelty in higher education. There's a certain cosmopolitan flavor to her experiences.")

After she had completed her master's degree, Mertie found herself at the crossroads of a career choice. "I didn't know what I was going to do," she confesses. Then unexpectedly, "out of the blue," she received word that there was an opening for a professor of home economics at the University of Minnesota. "It sometimes happens that way—out of the blue—that life changes course," Mertie observes sagely. She applied for the position and was hired. She taught home economics for five years, then decided "it was time to move on."

It was during this teaching period that Mertie met Stanley Buckman, her future husband. "It was in a butcher shop," she recalls. "I was teaching summer school, and Stanley was a graduate student, working on his Ph.D. in forestry. Apparently, he saw me in the butcher shop and was interested, so he asked the butcher for my name." She smiles, wrapped in recollection. "That afternoon, I had been out riding horseback and had just gotten home when the phone rang."

"Is this Mertie Willigar?" a male voice asked.

"I said, 'Yes,' but the caller hung up! I assume he was checking to see if he had the correct telephone number. Then the phone rang again, and it was Stanley Buckman, asking if he could come over and if I would like to go for a ride." She explains that, at this time, dating was a money-conscious undertaking, consisting of rides in borrowed cars, long walks, and shared ice-cream cones. "I told him to give me some time to change, as I had just come in off horseback, and he came calling a bit later."

Mertie's first date with the future Dr. Buckman consisted of riding in a borrowed car to a pole-yard, where Stanley had a graduate assistantship treating telephone poles with creosote to preserve the wood. "I remember thinking, 'Golly, what a funny first date,'" she laughs. Obviously, that date—or something in the young man's demeanor or character—made a favorable impression, because she continued to date Stanley Buckman. The couple shared a mutual acquaintance, one of Stanley's supervising professors who was a University of Washington alumnus, so that association furthered their early relationship.

"I had been going with someone else before I met Stanley," she confides. "But he had no goals, no plans for marriage and career, and I thought it over quite a bit."

Mertie admits that she had always wanted to marry and have children. "Most young girls do, don't you think? I was attracted to Stanley because he had

strong interests. He knew what he wanted, what he hoped to accomplish when he was finished with school." She describes her future husband as a young man who was driven to succeed, who "secretly wanted to be a doctor," but he realized there wasn't enough money for him to complete the required, extensive training in medical school and hospital residency. His alternative was to complete a doctor of philosophy degree in forestry and biochemistry. "Stanley was earnest and interested, and I chose him," she smiles. After a brief pause, she adds, "And I wasn't sorry."

Marriage

Mertie Willigar and Stanley Buckman were married August 19, 1933, in the home of his parents, John Joseph and Mabel Dodge Buckman, in Madelia, Minnesota. The country was mired in the midst of the Great Depression (1929-1939), and the national economy had hit rock-bottom just as Franklin D. Roosevelt became President six and a half months earlier. As unemployment soared to 15 million—with additional millions working for mere subsistence wages—the outlook was not hopeful for the young couple. But Mertie, 29 years old, and Stanley, 25 years old, possessed the youthful conviction that all things are possible if pursued with a strong will and an optimistic vision for the future.

With their marriage taking place on the stage of the Great Depression, the young couple had no assurance of a livelihood. They hoped that Stanley's employment would continue with the American Creosoting Company, with whom Stanley held a fellowship while he was in graduate school, but the fellowship had not been renewed by their marriage date. When the fellowship was later renewed, they moved to Toledo, Ohio, where Stanley began his first appointment as a post-doctoral fellow with American Creosoting Company.

Their residence in Toledo was "unappealing… because of the heat," according to Mertie. "The only advantage in Toledo was that we were able to buy tenderloin steak for 18 cents a pound!" In 1933, she points out, a surplus supply of beef was newsworthy, both as a dilemma for suppliers and a blessing for consumers.

After their first summer in Toledo, Mertie returned to Minnesota to teach another school year, while Stanley moved to the company headquarters in Louisville, Kentucky. There he developed a research laboratory for American Creosoting and engaged in a number of field trips for the company. The Buckmans lived apart during this year, being reunited during vacations. "And so I early became used to his traveling," Mertie comments, acknowledging an initial independence in her marriage relationship, as well as an expectation that Stanley would devote himself to his work.

After her teaching year in Minnesota was completed, Mertie joined her husband in Louisville in 1935. She accepted a position on the faculty of the home economics department of the University of Louisville, where she taught until the first Buckman son, Robert Henry (nicknamed "Bob" and called "Bobby" in childhood), was born in 1937. A little over two years later, the second Buckman son, John Dustin, was born in 1940. As with all young mothers, Mertie's first years with her babies required around-the-clock stamina, in addition to her duties as wife and homemaker.

During the family's five years in Louisville, Stanley and a college-era friend, Dale Chapman, who was selling chemicals for Dow Chemical Company, discussed Dale's idea for their setting up an independent chemical company. He had approached Stanley with the argument that "I'm selling material for wood preservation, and you *know* wood preservation, so why don't we team up? Stanley, you mix 'em, and I'll sell 'em!" The entrepreneur in Stanley Buckman responded to the challenge, and they agreed that Stanley would run the factory production while Dale traveled to sell the product. As plans developed, they chose Memphis as the site for their new venture for a number of reasons: The riverport offered natural resources and a network of transportation systems; the federal New Deal program, the Tennessee Valley Authority (TVA)—created by the Congress in 1933 to control flooding in seven southern states and develop low-cost electrical power for the area—would provide economical utility rates; the cost of labor would be relatively inexpensive; and the mild to warm Delta climate would be conducive to year-round production.

Thus, Stanley Buckman and Dale Chapman entered into partnership and opened their initial facility, named Central Laboratories, on Brooks Road in Memphis. Those early days of Central Laboratories were long and arduous ones, with the work accomplished by two employees in a rented, makeshift factory. "You know, around a chemical company, a lot of things can happen," Mertie comments. At one point, there was a small explosion at the factory, followed by a fire, and the office was moved into the Buckman home for a brief period. "We shared many talks then, about whether we should go on…was it worth it? Was it a good idea? Stanley had definite ideas about business, so we kept going."

A Growing Company

By 1945, Stanley Buckman's "definite ideas about business" had proven successful for the fledgling company. That year, the Buckmans sold their half of the enterprise (by now known as Chapman Chemical), secured a loan to supplement their profit from the business, and began their own company. For their new business, they purchased property on North McLean in Memphis, where now stands the international headquarters of Buckman Laboratories.

Mertie is characteristically matter-of-fact when she speaks of the past life-altering business decisions. "I suppose you always ask yourself, 'What might happen?' But we thought, 'Well, we can chance it, and if we lose, we've lost nothing but money; we haven't lost anything else. And we could start doing something

else.' There were several times when we wondered if we had done the right thing…should we go on? But you know the old saying, 'If you risk nothing, you gain nothing.'"

The new property on McLean consisted of 12 acres of weed-infested land and "a very, very dirty house," Mertie recalls, shaking her head as she remembers the long, dirty chore of cleaning the property and the equally time-consuming task of setting up offices and a laboratory. "The first tank we set up was a 55-gallon reactor in the basement; on the floor above were the offices and a library…not much of a library," she chuckles, "but there were a few books, so we could say that was the start of a library and laboratory facilities." During the first year, the Buckmans hired Bill Stitt as their first marketing person. "Bill took a risk, too, at the time, to leave his job at Thompson Haywood to join us. We also had a young man working for us, a chemist named Bob Meals. We hired a secretary, but she knew nothing about bookkeeping…," she recalls, pausing to shake her head as she recalls that early situation, then adds, "so I helped with that. We kept very primitive records in those early days."

Those early days of Buckman Laboratories were beneficiaries of Stanley Buckman's business and chemical acumen combined with Mertie's keen attention to organization and details. The first product developed by Buckman Laboratories in the small basement reactor was a fungicide for controlling molds, slime, and bacteria in the paper mills. It was called BSM-11. "Perhaps the name of the first product came from the initials of our names—Buckman, Stitt, and Meals—or perhaps it came from the initials for bacteria, slime, and molds…take your choice," Mertie conjectures wryly. The company's first order "came in on my birthday on October 19, 1945," from Whiting Paper Company in Holyoke, Massachusetts, a manufacturer of fine paper. It was a "red-letter" day for the company and the family. The order was for 200 gallons of the fungicide, so they put the 55-gallon reactor (which she sometimes refers to as a "kettle") to work.

In the summer of 1946, Mertie and Stanley took the first of their summer trips into northern Minnesota, Wisconsin, and Canada to visit paper mills and make product presentations. "We had a microscope and petri dishes with us," she explains, "and we would take samples of the liquids produced during the papermaking process in the various places to prove there was a need for our product. At night, we'd count the number of colonies in the petri dish and report back the next morning to the mill managers." Mertie's explanations are precise, then she arches an eyebrow and grins wryly, "And I thought, 'Well, is this going to work or isn't it?'"

Marjorie and Bill Stitt (left), friends of Mertie (right) since 1945, when Bill Stitt became the first marketing person for the fledgling Buckman Laboratories, frequently offer Memphis' First Lady of Philanthropy a respite of rest and recreation at their home in Anacortes, Washington.

Photograph from personal collection of Mertie Buckman

It worked, and Buckman Laboratories began to receive a steady stream of orders. The business was incorporated in 1946, and its list of products began to expand. Expansion fueled the need for additional chemists, and John Pera, a former employee of Central Labs who had just returned from military service in World War Two, was hired. He would later become vice president for research and development, as well as a member of the board of directors. Dr. Pera's affiliation with Buckman Laboratories and his continuing education at Christian Brothers College established an early association between the company and CBU, which continues to the present time.

The early years were not without incident; there was another chemical fire and a later, more serious explosion. "We had setbacks, and money was tight," Mertie admits. "In private, we would talk about whether we should move out and sell the company, or borrow money and how to pay it back…what to do." Mertie's memory of the fire of 1947 is vivid. "It was March second, on a Sunday morning," when one of their neighbors called to say the place was on fire. Someone driving by the factory had seen flames, blown the automobile's horn to attract the neighbors' attention, and called the fire department. The fire fighters came quickly, broke into the building, and extinguished the fire. While battling the blaze, the men hastily shoveled papers out the office window, "which we were sorry to see afterward," she notes with regret, since some research reports were lost. The overall damage, however, was minimal, and the cause of the fire was quickly discovered; the faulty valves on the furnace were promptly replaced. The fire "didn't stop Stanley," she says, and production was soon resumed. "We established a company policy, after the fire, that all the office doors were to be closed at night."

During the following two years, 1947 and 1948, the Buckmans began thinking about "meeting people and seeing how things could be developed on a worldwide basis," Mertie recalls, citing Stanley's initial visits, with a Portuguese dictionary for translation assistance, to tanneries in Brazil. They traveled together to Europe in the summer of 1947, stopping in New York, Newfoundland, Iceland, and Copenhagen for refueling the propeller-driven airplanes. "That first year we went to visit paper mills in Sweden, Norway, Finland, Belgium, France, and Switzerland to meet people who were corresponding with Stanley, and

The first site of Buckman Laboratories, purchased in 1945 on North McLean in Memphis, consisted of 12 weed-infested acres of land and a "very, very dirty house" which was cleaned and transformed into the company's first offices, library, and laboratory
Photograph courtesy of Buckman Laboratories, Memphis.

sometimes we met new people."

Mertie's recollections of these trips reveal glimpses of her life-long enjoyment of new experiences, her appreciation for cultural differences, and her compassion for those in need. She speaks of the high price of coffee in Finland after the war's conclusion and of political tensions between the Finnish and the Russians. She describes the contents of a folk museum in Sconsin, Sweden, and recalls with delight a woman who was the director of a Helsinki museum and with whom she shared mutual interest in the textiles exhibit; the woman later invited Mertie to her home for a visit. "When we returned to Memphis, we sent 'care' packages of coffee and sugar to the mills that we visited, as well as to my friend at the museum, along with some clothing…all of which were in short supply after the war."

At the end of the decade, in 1949, a serious explosion occurred at the Buckman plant on North McLean, casting the company's continued operation in a precarious position. "A gasket gave way on one of the reactors," Mertie recalls. Fortunately, the workers on site realized that something was wrong, so a general evacuation order was issued; everyone had left the building before the explosion, so no one was hurt. "But as the gasket blew, it blew out the roof and the side of the building, and there was a lot of damage."

At the time of the explosion, Stanley Buckman was in Cuba investigating the feasibility of expanding the company's products into the sugar-mills market. He returned to Memphis the day after the accident, and Mertie and the boys met his flight at the airport. She had previously warned her two sons not to greet their father with the bad news, saying, "Let him get home first and get settled." She laughs as she visualizes that airport scene. "But you know children: bad news, as well as

As Buckman Laboratories expanded its markets for chemical products in the 1960s and 1970s, Mertie often accompanied her husband, Stanley, on trips abroad. She was photographed during a dinner in Japan in September, 1966.

Photograph from the personal collection of Mertie Buckman.

good news, can't be kept," and so the first thing the excited boys said was, "Dad, we had an explosion!"

Stanley Buckman was inundated by descriptions of the plant explosion from his family, neighbors, plant personnel, and the news media. The January 21, 1949, headline of the Memphis *Press-Scimitar* announced in large, bold letters: "**7 Men Flee Building: Then the Explosion! Mighty Blast Shakes City.**" The newspaper account includes reports of the repercussions of the plant explosion, with nearby construction workers being hit by flying debris and structures' windows being blown out as far away as Rugby Park. Callers to the police and fire stations reported feeling vibrations from the explosion in South Memphis, Frayser, and Woodstock, 18 miles north of Memphis. At the damaged plant, "steel girders and pipes inside were twisted like wire[s]."

The newspaper's graphic account of the seven employees who "escaped with their lives" ignited public response to the explosion. The plant's neighbors became fearful of the potential danger of living near a chemical plant, and several nearby residents circulated a petition to prevent the plant's rebuilding. "So, Stanley called Bill Stitt, who was up in Chicago at the time, and said, 'Come back, we've got a public-relations job to do.' They had meetings with the neighbors, sometimes in group meetings at the company and sometimes by going house to house to talk," recounts Mertie. The public-relations campaign was successful and most of the neighbors eventually signed a petition stating that they would like to see the plant rebuilt, and a building permit was issued.

A *Press-Scimitar* editorial statement on February 26, 1949, includes some details of the extent of Dr. Buckman's public-relations effort, as well as his sense of responsiblity to the community. The editors praise Buckman Laboratories for its construction plans, which included explosion-proofing the building with a layer of roofing that would contain any future explosion without causing damage to the area surrounding the plant. In addition, the company voluntarily offered restitution for any loss to homeowners, should they be forced to sell their homes at less than market value as a result of the explosion. The restitution agreement was in effect for up to two years following the accident. In closing the statement, the editors praise Dr. Buckman's contribution to the stabilization of employment in Memphis after the war, through his work as a member of the city's committee for economic development.

Although Mertie says little of the public-relations problems involved in operating a chemical-manufacturing plant, it becomes obvious that the history of Buckman Laboratories is not without controversy. Neighbors were concerned about their property values and potential physical dangers created by the manufacture of chemicals; organized unions and their labor negotiators required considerable effort and compromise over the years; and the company's interests in South Africa were criticised during the 1980s, as media coverage of the Republic of South Africa's policy of apartheid was revealed to Americans through accounts of violent antiapartheid protests for racial reforms. "It is to Mertie's credit that she continued her philanthropic efforts in the community, sometimes anonymously, even though a lesser woman might have had resentments toward the neighborhood," notes Gid Smith of the Community Foundation. He points out that Mertie contributed matching funds toward a neighborhood development project in the early 1990s to benefit the neighborhood that once protested against her family's business.

After the 1949 explosion, Buckman Laboratories resumed production by erecting a tent on the site to allow construction of the new plant on a 24-hour-a-day schedule, despite the winter weather. During this rebuilding, the company borrowed laboratory space from Rhodes College, then Southwestern at Memphis, at the invitation of Dr. Rhodes, the college's president. "The college offered space to Dr. Buckman to use after classroom hours," recalls Loyd Templeton, assistant to the president of Rhodes, "and that association began a long-time friendship between the college and the company that has grown over the years."

As Mertie recounts the early history and milestones of Buckman Laboratories, it is difficult to reconcile tales of basement reactors and devastating chemical accidents with the present multinational company producing over 900 products and employing over 1200 persons or to equate those early years with the vast corporation that is now Bulab Holdings, Inc., the holding company, and its associated companies, including Buckman Laboratories—the manufacturing and distributing entity—and Buckman Laboratories International—the research, development, and consulting entity.

Yet, the milestones offer tangible evidence of the company's phenomenal progress: Buckman enterprises expanded into Canada in 1948 and reached the million-dollar-sales figure in 1949; the company purchased and operated a mine for raw materials from 1951 until 1958; it expanded into Mexico and Belgium in 1963, then into Australia, Brazil, and South Africa in 1971; it expanded into Monaco and Germany in 1984, then to the United Kingdom in 1985; it reached the 100-million-dollar-sales figure in 1987 and expanded into Argentina, Spain, and Japan, then into Austria in 1988; and in this decade of the 1990s it has expanded into Portugal, New Zealand, Italy, Singapore, Uruguay, Sweden, and Malaysia.

While thoughtfully contemplating Stanley Buckman's drive and unparalleled energy, Jim Daughdrill asks with astonished admiration, "Can you even imagine the vision of this man? He and Mertie just took off and went into new countries, not speaking the language, with few connections, and made it happen. At that time, it wasn't as easy to travel, and international business was in its infancy. It's truly amazing and gives you some idea of the quality of Stanley's vision…his undaunted willingness to try new ventures and make things happen."

Mertie also has been surprised by the company's growth, although not by the dedication of her husband to make it successful. "I knew that Stanley had his ideas and his drive, and I had a sense that he would do well. But I really didn't know that the company would grow to such an extent as this," she admits. "Stanley loved his work, loved what he did…he would be proud."

*Current home of Buckman Holding Company and Buckman Laboratories
on North McLean in Memphis, TN.*
Photograph courtesy of Buckman Laboratories.

Dr. Stanley J. Buckman
Photograph from personal collection of Mertie Buckman.

Dr. Stanley J. Buckman

Dr. Stanley J. Buckman (1909-1978) most certainly would have been proud of the multinational corporation given birth by the original Buckman Laboratories formed in Memphis in 1945. And Mertie Willigar Buckman, who shared his life for 46 years as a supportive partner, helpmate, wife, and mother of their two sons, offers choice insights into this irrepressible man.

With the passage of 20 years since Stanley Buckman's death, Mertie long ago reached emotional acceptance of having discovered her husband, dead of natural causes, in his office on Sunday morning, September 10, 1978. "We had been preparing for this [the possibility of sudden death], in a way," she says quietly. Dr. Buckman had been in failing health in the 1970s, being both overweight and over-stressed, yet he stubbornly refused to see a physician about his health. He continued to relentlessly press forward with his work, continuing a long-established pattern of often working around-the-clock. "It wasn't unusual for him to spend the night at the office," Mertie recalls, so she wasn't worried when Dr. Buckman failed to return home that September weekend in 1978. By late Saturday, however, she began to have a slight feeling of uneasiness when she couldn't reach him by telephone. "We had a new man on security [watch], and he wasn't able to give me any information by phone on Saturday." Her lingering feeling of vague misgiving prompted Mertie to go to his office Sunday morning to check on him, and there she found her husband's lifeless body.

"It was better that I found him on Sunday, because Bob had been out of town on Saturday, and on Sunday he was available and could take care of matters," she says in a quiet, matter-of-fact voice. For a while she seems wrapped in memories of coping with that September shock and abrupt loss.

The September 11, 1978, issue of the Memphis *Commercial Appeal* provides some of the details of Dr. Buckman's sudden death and previous achievements. A photograph of the man, accompanied by a starkly bold headline proclaiming "**Stanley Buckman, 69, Found Dead,**" captures the image of a heavy-set, suit-clad businessman with sternly impressive features, looking directly and frankly into the camera's lens. The obituary chronicles his co-founding in 1941 of Central Laboratories, Inc., and his founding in 1945 of Buckman Laboratories, Inc., as well as his holding more than 40 patents for his chemical work and having published more than 40 scientific papers. Also listed in the notice were numerous professional achievements, including his election as a fellow of the American Association for the Advancement of Science in 1967 and as a fellow of the American Institute of Chemists in 1969, and the description of Stanley Buckman as "a pioneer in the control of pollution with chemicals." His friends and colleagues describe him in more personal terms. Jim Daughdrill, president of Rhodes College (then named Southwestern), where Dr. Buckman was elected to the board of trustees in 1967 and elected a trustee for life in 1978, said he was a "man of moral dignity and strength, a person you had to visit in his office in order to see the simplicity and order that comes from a creative scientific mind." He described Dr. Buckman as a man who maintained "the enthusiasm of a 20-year-old during his entire life." He also noted that Stanley Buckman had been a generous contributor to Southwestern (now Rhodes) and a library in the science complex was named in his honor. Dr. Buckman's office staff were quoted as remembering that their "Boss" had taken only one vacation away from Buckman Laboratories and that was "a cruise several years ago the staff paid for as a Christmas gift." Upon returning to Memphis, he commented that he had "just as soon be working in the office" and that the most interesting part of his trip had been "examining the boilers on board ship"—a task that related to his work.

Family members have similar impressions of Stanley Buckman's single-minded dedication to his work. His son, Robert, quickly observes that his father was "as stubborn a man as you'll ever meet." The expression on Bob's face speaks volumes as he recounts his father's failing health and his refusal to consult a physician. Dr. Buckman's granddaughter, Kathy Buckman Davis, recalls the summer she interned with the family business while Stanley Buckman was running the company. "It was one of my tasks to schedule the required employee physicals, and I noticed that Grandfather was due for a physical. I was attempting to schedule his appointment," she says, but to no avail; several of her co-workers, apparently aware of Dr. Buckman's penchant for avoiding anything he considered unimportant, merely shook their heads and wished her "good luck." The physical examination never was scheduled. At another point, Bob

recalls, they had arranged for the family physician to come to Stanley's office to insist upon a consultation...again, to no avail.

Dr. Buckman's strong-minded determination to do things his own way was legendary. "Stanley Buckman was what I would call a benevolent dictator," recalls Jim Daughdrill, who serves on the board of directors of Buckman Laboratories and was both friend and colleague to Stanley. "He was hands-on...I mean, he ran the place. He was paternalistic, but I mean this as a good thing: he *provided* for people."

In providing for his employees, Dr. Buckman instituted a company policy to never lay-off employees. "And I have to tell you," Dr. Daughdrill continues, "that, as a board member, I had trouble with that policy. It cost [the company] money." But Stanley Buckman was insistent that he would find a place for his employees, regardless of the fluctuations in the economy. He also insisted upon generous benefits for his employees, including matching funds for continuing education.

Dr. Buckman's paternalistic sense of responsibility for those he employed fostered a feeling of "family" among the employees of Buckman Laboratories. This familial attitude remains evident 20 years later in the company's employee newsletters and in the daily interaction among employees at the company headquarters. Members of the staff know and care for one another and are included in awards dinners, casual lunches, and family outings. In the fortieth-anniversary special edition of Buckman Laboritories' newsletter, a long-time employee, Frances Murphy, recalls the inclusive camaraderie of these parties. "There was no separation of the races," she writes. "Every employee received a Christmas bonus; every spouse, guest, and child [received] a gift under the Christmas tree. There was no other place in Memphis that we could hold such a gathering until the advent of desegregation after [the Civil Rights Act of June 29,] 1964."

Not only was Dr. Buckman a benevolent provider, "he was a great thinker," observes Jim Daughdrill. He decided to encourage creativity on the job by providing each employee with a little green notebook, in which they were to jot down ideas for more efficient performance or for changes that would benefit the company and its customers. These notebooks were called "idea traps" and were distributed to all Buckman employees.

Stanley Buckman was a man of eccentricities and novel ways of thinking. "He was quite interested in the process of aging as he became older," Jim recalls. He researched and attended meetings focusing on the investigation of freezing tissue and prolonging life. He also investigated the effects of vitamins, and he and Mertie took vitamin supplements in paste form. ("This was disgusting stuff," remembers granddaughter Kathy Davis, with a grimace.)

Stanley and Mertie Buckman celebrated their 25th wedding anniversary on August 19, 1958.
Photograph from personal collection of Mertie Buckman.

"He had a scientific, resourceful mind, one that encouraged the attitude of 'inventor' in every employee," continues Jim Daughdrill. "He was so dominant, so in charge, such a powerful figure" that, until his death, it wasn't obvious that Mertie Buckman had her own separate, powerful presence. "He was so dominant, and she was so unobtrusive, that you just tended not to notice other people when Dr. Buckman was around." Although Jim does not know any details of the personal relationship between the senior Buckmans, it was obvious to him that Mertie was a constant, supportive presence for her husband. "He *relied* upon her, that was sure," he concludes.

Jane Himes, formerly the personal assistant to Dr. Buckman, observes that often in the course of decision-making at the office, Stanley would approach a difficult decision with the comment to her that he would "talk to Mertie about it." Mrs. Buckman demurs when asked about her influence at Buckman Laboratories—"It was really his company, so I left the running of the business up to him."—but the impression given in multiple interviews is that she was a powerful, albeit behind-the-scenes, influence.

At times, however, Mertie assumed a more public role in developing the business. When Buckman Laboratories was expanding into Canada in the late 1940s, she accompanied her husband on summer automobile trips through the countryside. They spent time in the pulp and paper mills, analyzing bacteria and fungicide counts to determine what Buckman Laboratories chemical products might provide benefit to the mills. "We would send the boys to spend some time with their grandparents in Minnesota, then travel for weeks calling on customers. Of course, I went along," she says modestly.

In early 1960s, Buckman Laboratories expanded into Belgium. Mertie traveled with her husband, Stanley, to assist with setting up new offices. She conducted employee interviews in her hotel room and typed important papers on a portable typewriter balanced on her knees.
Photograph courtesy of Buckman Laboratories, Memphis.

Later, when Buckman Laboratories' expansion into Belgium was underway in the early 1960s, Mertie accompanied her husband to Belgium, conducting employee interviews in her hotel room and typing important documents on a portable typewriter balanced on her knees. She followed the same routine in Mexico in 1963. "Some very important papers were typed on my typewriter," she says, "sometimes while I perched on the bed, typing late into the night."

Recalling the business trips with her husband 35 years ago, Mertie reveals that she "got a glimpse of my husband during that trip to Belgium that I had not seen before. I saw the way that men do business, and this was a new world to me." Her awareness and observation of the differences between men and women added depth to the insightful perceptions already stored within Mertie and, in all probability, reinforced her advocacy for women's empowerment first inspired by her mother's unfulfilled yearning for education.

Through a domestic anecdote, Mertie provides further illumination of her relationship with Stanley Buckman. "I remember that, early after we had moved into our home in Lakewood, I mentioned to Stanley that I wanted a heater in the bathroom. And he said 'no,' we didn't need that." She didn't argue—"What would have been the point?"—and quietly accepted his pronouncement. A short while later, however, when he was away on a business trip, she had the bathroom-heater installed. Upon his return home from his trip, "he never said a word about it," she smiles.

Mertie Buckman, who grew into adulthood at a time when women were expected to serve within narrowly confined roles, developed a talent for quiet independence during her marriage to Stanley Buckman. Her self-assured independence has been hard-won, yet she remains a very feminine woman who has reared a family, nurtured a husband as well as a company, and supported a community. In terms of the women's rights movement revived in the 1970s, would she call herself a feminist? She considers this conformity to labeling of personal convictions, then nods slowly. "It's not a label that I use, but…yes, I would say that I am."

Robert Buckman grins as he applies retrospective to his parents' ostensible marital relationship and his mother's independence. "That's what she's all about, being independent. It was always her way," he says with a mixture of admiration and affection. And did he also perceive his father as a "paternalistic, benevolent dictator," as described by Jim Daughdrill? "Oh, he was a powerful man and very much into controlling his business," he says, but apparently Stanley Buckman's paternalistic control did, indeed, extend to his immediate family. "Dad made arrangements in his will that we were to inherit trust funds at age 30, but only if we were either involved in the running of the business or were actively pursuing training or education to contribute to our joining the business." Bob adds that the terms of the will also extend to the grandchildren. "I think of it as the heavy hand of Stanley Buckman extending even from the grave," he says, with a shade of irony. "Dad wanted to ensure continued family involvement in the company." He continues by saying that his own parenting philosophy differs markedly from his father's. "Dad was putting boxes around us. I don't see it that way; I'd rather open windows than draw boxes," he points out, then shrugs his shoulders. "Each of us is different."

Bob explains, and perhaps attempts to justify, his father's need for control and his relentless drive by sharing some of the Buckman history. Stanley was the older of two sons, who grew up working on the family farm in Minnesota. There was only enough money in the family coffers for one son to go to college, so Stanley, the firstborn, was chosen for higher education. His younger brother, Russell, apparently felt he received short shrift in the arrangement, so Stanley was determined that the money—by birth right—expended for his education be put to good use. "So he felt he *had* to succeed, there was no choice but to succeed. He was *driven*." Stanley's drive to succeed was accompanied by an inventive, visionary mind, enabling him to diligently immerse himself in work for 16 to 18 hours each day. "I won't do that," Bob states emphatically. "Dad had trouble turning loose of stuff, [he] couldn't let go so that the company could expand. That's what we've done here in the last two decades, and the company has grown in a phenomenal way." Could his father have foreseen the future of the company? Bob doubts it. "He had to be in control, so he could see only as far as he could personally manage," he observes thoughtfully. "Of course, that was pretty far."

Dr. Buckman's need for control also extended to his own health, to his detriment. "He thought he knew more than the doctors, which is always dangerous," Bob says regretfully, remembering his father's death in 1978. "He was a difficult man in many ways, but brilliant." After a moment's silent introspection, he adds, "When Dad died, Mother was really thrust into deciding how to make a difference financially."

He explains that, upon Stanley's death, Mertie inherited a trust fund that has continued to grow. "I told her then that she could either give it away now and have a hand in it, or wait [for disbursement] 'til she died, then the government would decide where it went." He pauses to chuckle, his expression implying that her choice of the former option is obvious. "So, she's thrown herself into her philanthropic work. She chooses projects and acts as a steward, making gifts and following through with organizations she supports."

The widowed Mrs. Buckman has applied herself as diligently to philanthropic support of community improvement as Dr. Buckman applied himself to building Buckman Laboratories. And our society has been greatly enhanced by the visionary efforts of both Stanley and Mertie Buckman.

Mrs. S. J. Buckman and Family

"Mrs. S. J. Buckman" is the title identifying Mertie in the early newspaper clippings recording her community involvement in the 1950s and 1960s. The large collection of press clippings catalogued at Buckman Laboratories invariably includes photographs of her alone or in groups of women gathered for coffees and teas. Mertie's campaign for the creation of the Raleigh branch of the public library is chronicled, as is her volunteerism in behalf of the Young Women's Christian Association, the Church Women United, the American Association of University Women, and the National Conference of Christians and Jews. These photographs capture an attractive middle-aged woman, simply but impeccably attired, who has joined the ranks of similar women to give of her time and resources for civic causes, having in common with other women the dual responsibilities of rearing children and supporting businessmen-husbands. What is not revealed in these newspaper accounts is the private person behind the good works.

Aside from her public persona, who was she? Who was this woman who worked quietly in the community for decades while she packed school lunches, rounded up her two sons for dinner, went over business decisions with her husband, made phone calls to her friends, and organized women to extend their influence into the community?

Mertie is reticent when asked to describe herself as a mother. She acknowledges that she reared her sons with a sense of responsibility and encouraged them to become independent individuals. "You can't do everything for children; you have to let them decide things and do for themselves," she comments. "I had high expectations of my children, and, on occasion, I stepped in and insisted on some things." Her personal style of leadership, however, has leaned more toward influence than insistence. Her own strong sense of individualism and independence lends credence to the assumption that her style of mothering includes modeling by example, rather than by lecturing. She is a woman of calm action and economy of words.

During Mertie's young-adult years filling the roles of homemaker and mother of two active boys, she actively supported numerous school activities and nurtured her affinity for nature and horticulture through membership in the Weeders and Seeders Garden Club. Many lasting friendships were formed with women engaged in similar pursuits during this period, and her female friends remain loyal in their affection and memories of Mertie's good nature and strength of spirit.

One long-time friend and former neighbor is Alma Pierotti, whose husband Harry, a Memphis probate judge, died in 1975. The Pierottis were neighbors of the Buckmans when the families lived on Kendale in the 1940s, before the Buckmans built their home in Lakewood. Alma Pierotti, a petite woman who speaks

Mertie Willigar Buckman and Stanley J. Buckman with their sons Robert (left) and John (right).
Photograph from personal collection of Mertie Buckman.

in the slow drawl of the Deep South, reminisces fondly. "Our backyards connected at a shared gate, and my two sons and her two boys played together," she recalls. She describes Mertie as a dear friend whom she has always admired, as well as being a kindred spirit who joined with her in sharing their boys' misadventures. "Bobby was a real rascal," she laughs, describing how one day the four boys ventured farther from home than their mothers would have allowed, over to the Parkway and into the pastures where horses grazed. "They never should have been so far from home. But late that afternoon, here came the four boys walking down our street with a horse in tow! We were beside ourselves, because they had taken someone's horse, for heaven's sake, but they claimed the horse had just followed them home." Alma Pierotti is relishing the retelling of this family tale, and adds, "I called to Mertie to come see what our sons had dragged home *this time*. I was just exasperated. But she was so good; she just tied up that horse in her yard. The next day we put an ad in the newspaper, advertising for whoever lost a horse to come get it."

Alma smiles in recollection. "The boys were free to roam, and they were always getting into some devilment. Mertie and I would smooth things over. They'd bring home cats and dogs and snakes. I never liked that at all. Although Mertie didn't seem to mind the snakes so much, I'd have a fit if they brought those snakes to me!" Alma explains that she and Mertie were quite different as mothers, although they got along well. Alma's style was more strict and traditional—"no feet on the coffee table" and "no slimy things in the house." Mertie was more likely to share their delight in their discoveries of small creatures and in outdoor experiments. "Mertie would correct the boys, of course, but I never once saw her lose her temper," recalls Alma. "She was more relaxed, somewhat more permissive. She was a bit older when she became a mother than I had been—that may have had something to do with it. And she was never shy about saying how old she was, either. She didn't mind when the boys pointed out her gray hair."

Mertie with her sons. John (left) and Bob (right), in the mid-1970s.
Photograph from personal collection of Mertie Buckman.

Alma remembers Stanley Buckman as a man who was "all business, but quite nice," although she confesses, "I didn't really know him well. We [the two couples] didn't really mix socially, since our husbands' fields were so entirely different." Mertie and Alma shared confidences and borrowed household items from each other.

40

Alma remembers being embarrassed one afternoon when Dr. Buckman came looking for Mertie, and Alma had the contents of her "junk drawer" strewn about the kitchen. The two women looked after each other's childen and often treated all four boys to an early dinner. Bobby, as Alma recalls, would be the Buckman son most likely to get into trouble for jumping on the furniture. "John played more quietly," she remembers, less like his father than Bobby.

Alma Pierotti mentions an additional connection with the Buckmans: one of her husband's relatives, John Pera, was an early employee of Buckman Laboratories. "John Pera was graduated from Christian Brothers, and Dr. Buckman sent John on to Southwestern and then to get his doctorate; he eventually moved way up in Buckman Laboratories." She then reminisces on the growth of the company, on how life in the city has changed ("some of it not for the better"), the loss of husbands, and the birth of grandchildren. She also remembers how Mertie encouraged her friends to become involved in community affairs. "When the Conference of Christians and Jews was forming, Mertie called me and asked me to join. 'Alma, she said, I want you to join us. You can represent the Catholics.' I was not sure about this, and I told her, 'You're always so involved, even with two children, but I'm not sure I can.' But she said they needed me, so I finally agreed." She pauses to consider Mertie's total involvement in life, then says with admiration, "I always knew she was smart, but I had no idea she would accomplish so much—helping with the business, serving on boards of directors…" Alma's voice trails off as memories preoccupy her thoughts. Perhaps she is searching through scenes from those early years and trying to connect the thread to mature Mertie, civic leader and philanthropist, from young Mertie, loving and tolerant mother of two active sons.

Mertie's having embarked upon motherhood beyond the traditional just-out-of-school age for women in the South—giving birth at age 33 to her first son—and her having borne the Deep South social stigma of New Hampshire "Yankee" when she relocated in Louisville, then Memphis (to face the challenge of forming friendships with females reared in the conservative Bible-belt culture of the South), offer new dimensions for exploration. How did her possessing such cultural "oddities" affect Mertie when she and her family set down new roots in the South in the mid-1930s?

"It was something of a culture shock," Mertie laughs, remembering the first year after she joined husband Stanley in Louisville in 1935. Her joining the faculty of the home economics department of the University of Louisville, where she taught classes in nutrition and interior decorating (the latter class furnished a model kitchen in Louisville's nine-day Home Show in the winter of 1936), assisted her in "developing an ear" for the language differences, but "I could sit right beside someone and engage in conversation, then not know what she was saying!" She recalls receiving a phone call during her first year in Louisville from a woman of some standing in the community, a woman "from a good family," who invited her to lunch. "I think she wanted to check me out…wanted to know what I looked like." Mertie ponders that social occasion with a bemused expression, then adds wryly, "I must have passed muster."

Although Mertie's acculturation was not instantaneous—and she retains a trace of her New Hampshire clipped, straight-forward speech and northern accent in certain vowels—her adaptation to the New South has been ongoing and *thorough*. "I got plenty of advice on how to manage my household. One thing I recall is that I was advised to never let my husband in the kitchen!" she laughs and shakes her head, obviously recalling other domestic mores firmly entrenched just before World War Two thrust American women into the war-munitions work force and redefined expectations for and by women.

"I had to get used to having a maid, since [domestic help] wasn't something I was used to, and I remember getting advice on managing household help." The rate of pay for house-maids was one dollar per day, commencing after breakfast and continuing until dinner time. "I paid more than that, and I was sure if I treated any woman working for me as a human being, then all would go well," she says, disparaging the common practice of the day of drawing lines between members of different social and racial classes.

Thinking back in time to picture his mother of some 55 years ago, Robert Buckman grins and quips, "What I remember is that she was always trying to get me to eat things I didn't like...Brussels sprouts, rutabaga!" He grimaces and shudders with revulsion. "She was a home-economics major, so she had *firm* ideas about nutrition."

After a moment of laughter, he approaches the subject of Mertie as mother with thoughtful reflection. "Well, I don't know...actually, she was just great. Growing up, I remember wishing I had more time with her, but she was wonderful because she was so involved and loved people. You know, she cares about

people—*really* cares about them—and was into YWCA and AAUW work [in Memphis after 1941] when I was in elementary school. For most of her life she's been interested in the whole range of women's issues...and for good reason," he says.

He rummages through his memory bank to recall some of his mother's early history: Mertie's responsibility for her sister and their traveling to the Pacific Northwest, her spending a summer in Europe as a student, and her work for a graduate degree. "She taught us to assume responsiblity, to be independent; those are instilled traits that directly affect how I do business," he says thoughtfully. "Mother has her own ideas about what's important, with an eye for the disadvantaged and the importance of education. She's really a change agent and makes things happen that might not have happened without her intervention," he observes, with familial pride and admiration reflected in his face.

In pulling from his mother-son memories, Bob recounts a favorite memory of the cross-country trip by automobile that he and his brother, John, took with their mother one summer from Memphis to California. "It was just great," he recalls. "We stopped along the way, collecting things and visiting people. By the time we got home, the car was filled to overflowing with rocks, plant clippings, and souvenirs. We had a grand time together."

Mertie vividly recalls that westward journey shared with her sons, commenting, "That would have been during the years when we had the mine operating. Stanley bought a mercury mine in California in 1951." The mine was located about 200 miles north of San Francisco, in Sonoma County and deep in the

Miacamus Mountains. Stanley's purchasing the mine "was a kind of insurance, because we needed mercury in some of our products, and we didn't want to be dependent upon suppliers," she explains, pointing out that mercury was in widespread industrial use at that time. (Mercury, a silver-colored metal sometimes called "quicksilver" because of its rapid flow, was mined from the ore cinnabar; California and Nevada have the largest cinnabar deposits in the contiguous United States. Mercury compounds were in popular use for antiseptics, ointments, fungicides, paint, and paper until the early 1970s.)

After Stanley Buckman bought the old Culver Bear mine, a good deal of effort was required to establish a mining town, since he had to locate several families who owned adjacent land in order to purchase the surrounding area. "He had quite a time of tracking people down. He finally hired a detective to find them all and then had to convince them to sell out to him," Mertie recalls. The mine was in a remote location, surrounded by steep and rugged mountainsides, so hauling mining equipment to the site was extremely difficult. Meeting the challenge head on, Stanley and his crew decided to break down the kiln into three parts for transporting through the mountains, then the convoy "snaked" along a goat track widened by a bulldozer; after a slow and tedious trek they succeeded in delivering the huge kiln to the mine. Once the equipment was reassembled and in place, the Buckmans tackled the equally difficult problem of providing accommodations and essential needs for the mine workers.

"The mine was 21 miles from the nearest town, along a very crooked and narrow mountain road, which washed out whenever it rained," Mertie recounts. "So, it was decided that we would need to build a community at the mine where we could house our employees. We ordered prefabricated housing…which, as was soon discovered, leaked and those roofing defects had to be fixed. We purchased a mess hall from an abandoned mine nearby; as with the kiln, it had to be cut into three pieces and hauled over the top of the mountain. I went over on one of the trips that brought it back." This building became the office and living quarters. The community housed 25 to 30 families and, since many of the miners' families included children, the Buckmans set up a school for the children. The local school board was persuaded to furnish a teacher, provided the company would supply the school building. "We had the only eight-grade, one-room schoolhouse in Sonoma County, but it was very satisfactory. The children were happy."

Mertie tells tales of mining-camp life with obvious enjoyment. The first summer, rattlesnakes were a problem, but that problem was solved by giving all the children cats to keep in the camp. After the cats chased off or ate the mice, the snakes moved on to follow their food source or find a new one. Traveling to and from the mine was extremely difficult, with the roads twisting and looping over the rugged mountain terrain, but Mertie learned to adroitly maneuver her automobile along the precipitous roads. In the mining camp, the Buckmans lived in a one-room cottage, called the "honeymoon cottage," with just the essential furnishings: a double-bed, a table utilized as a desk, a larger table for serving meals, and three folding chairs. "There were four of us, so one of us had to sit on the bed when we ate a meal," Mertie recalls. "We had an icebox—not an electric refrigerator—that we had to keep filled with blocks of ice, and a small stove. We sort of camped out. The boys slept on the porch, where they listened to the raccoons raid the garbage cans at night."

In concluding her tales of the mining camp, Mertie describes a woman who worked at the camp. "Her name was Dolly…Dolly Blakesly…and she was a very interesting person. (When Mertie describes any person as "interesting," it is typically a term of praise.) She had a colorful past: she had been a nurse on a battleship and had been married and divorced a couple of times. She had retired up in the hills, and we first met her when she was carrying mail along the mountain roads." After Dolly was hired to run the office in the mining camp, she "ran herd on everybody, especially the children, and looked after the office; she also took care that the drinking water was collected and treated. She helped beautify the camp by planting flowers and trees. She had a hillside by her house and carried loads and loads of dirt each day when she went home from work, until she finally had enough dirt there to plant flowers. Then [after her garden became productive], she would fuss about the deer coming into her garden to eat her flowers and vegetables at night." Mertie laughs and shakes her head as she remembers Dolly Blakesly.

The summers spent at the mining community were good times for Mertie and Stanley—days of productive work, problem-solving, and living with Mother Nature. And the mining venture was merely one in a long series of new frontiers for Stanley Buckman. Although he began by knowing little about mining, he quickly learned and acquired the necessary expertise as he went along…and Mertie went along, too. The courageous spirit of pioneers comes to mind, but Mertie denies feeling any such pioneering spirit. "I didn't feel very brave at the time," she says matter-of-factly. "It was just a normal thing to do." Normal, perhaps, for the Buckmans and for this remarkable woman who was reared to be independent, responsible, and resourceful.

Those traits instilled in Mertie by her parents also were nurtured in her sons. She began in their early youth to foster an awareness, a sense of recognition, in them for knowing "when to let go and let be." Bob Buckman readily admits that possessing the wisdom to willingly release control is difficult, although it's one of life's lessons he's been learning for many years. "It's taken me some time," he says reflectively, "but it's a lesson Mom learned early in life." He is referring to Mertie's youthful loss of her parents, but he also includes the loss of her husband in 1978 and, the following year, the loss of her younger son, John, by suicide.

John's death is rarely spoken of by members of the immediate family, whose collective psyche is indelibly imprinted with the tragedy. "We don't talk about it," quietly comments granddaughter Kathy Buckman Davis. "It's just too painful." A similar feeling of compassion is shared by family friends, who suffered for Mertie's sorrow following John's death in 1979, and long-time friend Dora Ivey admonishes that it's not a subject to explore with Mertie, since it will only sadden her. Yet, during a later interview, Mertie voluntarily discusses her feelings as a consequence of John's death, hoping that her experience will lend some solace to others who must endure this debilitating maternal pain. "I don't think children realize the effect of their actions on their parents," she says softly. She relates that John had been suffering from depression following his divorce, and she had encouraged him to seek counseling or participate in a support-group, but her entreaties were to no avail.

After the blessedly-numbing shock of her son's death began to subside, how did Mertie manage to deal with her grief? "She gritted it out," observes Brother Patrick O'Brien, and his four words speak volumes. Having inherited her New England foremothers' genetic "grit" of fortitude, their stoic acceptance of both natural and manmade disasters, Mertie set her backbone—if not her spirit—to "grit out" her devastating loss. Emotional pain prompts human beings to withdraw into protective shells to mask grieving (and Mertie is, indeed, a mortal human being), yet she finally began to find solace in giving to others and putting their interests before her own.

Over a long period of time, Mertie "learned to live with it. It does get better," she says in retrospect. "There was one thing I discovered...although I discovered it later than I might have...when I went to a meeting of AAUW, and there was a woman speaking on grief. It was so helpful to me to hear [of the feelings shared by] other women who had lost loved ones. It was a real comfort," she admits, and it was a welcome revelation to her that mutual sharing of pain lessened grief. "I'd want other women to know this, that sharing such things could be helpful."

Sharing feelings of grief in order to ease one's own burden and help another do the same was a journey through self-discovery for Mertie, who had built her life upon the strong virtues of independence, resourcefulness, and determination. Although those sterling qualities have not diminished with the passing of time, her hard-won awareness of her own vulnerability to pain and loss has strengthened and enriched her compassion for others. It also has developed deeper layers of sensitivity within the spiritual essence of Mertie.

Mertie Buckman hugs Campus School third-grader Jamal Fulton as Memphis City Schools' Adopt-A-School program helps partner Buckman Laboratories celebrate its 50th anniversary in 1995.

Photo: Copyright, 1995. *The Commercial Appeal*, Memphis, TN. Used with permission.

The Third Generation

Mertie's legacy of independence, resourcefulness, and determination is embodied in her granddaughter, Kathy Buckman Davis, who serves as general counsel to Buckman Laboratories. Kathy's inherent sense of responsibility is praised by those who know and work with her. Tom Southard, who works with her on the board of directors of St. Mary's Episcopal School, speaks highly of her abilities, and Nancy Cummins remarks that she sees in Kathy the strong influence of Mertie's civic responsibility. Barbara McConville observes that Kathy is a determined, professional woman.

Kathy Buckman Davis, who obtained her law degree from Emory Law School and was already a seasoned professional attorney in her thirties, joined Buckman Laboratories four years ago. What prompted her decision to join the family business, when she had been conducting a successful private practice in Atlanta? "I remember telling Dad [Bob Buckman] about my decision [to establish her law practice in Atlanta], and there was silence in response. I told him, 'Look, I'm no good to you 'til I've gone out on my own. Let me do this, then I'll consider joining the family business if the right opportunity arises.' So, that's the way it was," she says succinctly, "and I'm glad to be here, although I would have been happy staying in private practice. I never had definite plans to be at Buckman Laboratories."

And how does she feel about Stanley Buckman's will and his provisions for keeping family in the Buckman enterprises? "Oh, that's not all he did," she responds, and the attorney Kathy Davis begins a litany of provisions that Dr. Buckman included in employee contracts and company policy that attest to his eye toward the future of the company. Her grandfather's policies were formulated in a different time, and the "benevolent dictator" held different ideas about what the future would hold. "He wanted women in the family to inherit stock, but it was to be non-voting stock," she says, with an ironic smile and raised eyebrows.

The irony becomes evident as Kathy speaks of her role in the management of the business, as well as of her legacy from her grandfather. She sees in herself many of the characteristics of her strong grandfather—drive, determination, and vision for the future—so it's no wonder that Dr. Buckman's traditional view of women in business would rankle. Kathy's bristling against her grandfather's view of gender roles prompts thoughts of her grandmother's role as an advocate of women, which extends from a time in which expectations of women were narrowly construed. Echoes reverberate of one of Mertie's comments about her long history of community service and involvement in women's organizations during the time she was still managing a household with young children: "I was always involved and had my hand in the business, as well as in the YWCA and other organizations. My husband was good about it…he was nice enough to let me do it," Mertie had pointed out.

Although Kathy's generation of the late twentieth century has made considerable gains in gender equal-ity, she realizes her grandmother's statement reflects a Victorian concept that women were to be docile, domestically confined, and required to obtain permission from the controlling male (usually her husband or father) for any nonconforming behavior. Thus, Mertie and Kathy share separate histories as women with perspectives spanning from the beginning of this century to the end. Mertie's perspective offers a poignant reminder that the accomplishments of older women came at some cost. Dr. Buckman's tolerance of his wife's activities can be viewed, perhaps, as progressive for his time.

Mertie often comments on the benefits of women's abilities to find various creative outlets in their lives, to remain at home with their families while also taking part in the larger community, and to derive a sense of self separate from men's narrower confines of success in their chosen careers. "Men have a harder time [coping] when retirement comes, or when they lose their wives, or when business fails," she observes. "Women have had to adjust over the years to so many diffferent situations. They are more likely to have broader interests outside the home or their work, and they are better able to roll with the punches of life." A strength that women's traditional roles have offered them is the strength of friendship. "Women need to develop strong relationships with other women, and these relationships will serve them well," she advises. "Men already may have a 'good old boy network,' but women also need to develop networks of relationships that nurture them." She is quick to point out the need for women to call upon one another for mutual assistance and for establishing a sense of sisterhood. Mertie's sage observations are given additional worth by her own history of creating a sense of sisterhood through friendships formed during a time when women had fewer options for pursuing personal interests.

"Grandmother is a woman who is a product of her time, and her accomplishments are all the more remarkable for it," Kathy points out. "And I think after she became a widow, she sort of 'came into her own.' That's when her volunteer work [accelerated] and her philanthropy really became a force in the community. Of course, I'm sure it was a challenge for her."

Kathy smiles when asked about her "famous" grandmother. "It's hard for me to think of her as having some notoriety. It's not that she isn't remarkable—she's a vibrant woman who has wit and health and a sense of service into her late life—but she's *Grandmother*, you know?" And Kathy's memories lie in family gatherings during her childhood, while visiting in her grandparents' house. "The grandkids would stay overnight sometimes, and I remember she would let us drink *coffee!*" she chuckles, recalling her childish delight in being given that forbidden treat. "She'd let us doctor it up with cream and sugar…" After a moment of nostalgic reverie, she continues, "And I remember afternoons in her kitchen at Thanksgiving and Christmas, baking pies from scratch. We'd also make cranberry salad, using her old meat grinder to grind up the cranberries."

Mertie's granddaughter has firsthand knowledge of her active interests, her knowledge of current issues, and her eager pursuit of new and old friendships. "She can talk to anyone, sharing meaningful conversations with those who are 60 or 70 years her junior as easily as with her contemporaries. And keeping up with her just about wears me out," she laughs. Kathy recalls helping out at her grandmother's house over a long weekend, following Mertie's surgical removal of cataracts. "Although she was still recovering from the surgery, on the first morning I was there she showed me a list of things to do and places she needed me to take her. I blurted out, 'Grandmother, you've got to be kidding!'"

Mertie doesn't "kid" about needed tasks nor is she predisposed to give in to the demands of an aging body. Since her spirit has remained youthful and eager for new challenges, she pushes her body to keep pace with her active mind—often to the consternation of family members who are concerned for her health. "I remember that, even 10 years ago, Grandmother would get frustrated because she needed more sleep than she used to. I mean, she'd get frustrated that she'd naturally sleep on Saturday mornings 'til 8:30 or so…which was *late* for her," Kathy recalls with amazement. "We try to get her to take it easy and let go of some things that she's committed to, but it's hard to convince Grandmother of anything!"

This intergenerational struggle over the need for Mertie's slowing down has become an ongoing dynamic in the Buckman family. Mertie scoffs at their warnings. "Sometimes I think they want me to just *sit still*, but I'd rather wear out than rust out!" she exclaims with a soft, deprecating laugh that smoothes over some of her frustrations. Her strength of will to remain active is one of the core elements of Mertie Buckman's essence, and this tenacity—this stubbornness—is a trait inherent within the family. Kathy has her own stubborn streak and carries on the tradition-

al intergenerational dialogue with her grandmother concerning Kathy's independence. "I like to go out to the lake and take the boat out on my own, and Grandmother doesn't like that," Kathy says. "She wants me to take somebody with me." It's obvious that the determined struggle for independent choices is a two-way street.

The self-determination that characterizes generations of Buckmans is part of the legacy of Stanley Buckman. His death was a great loss to the family, but there is philosophical acceptance of the way he died. "We always knew he would die working," Kathy muses reflectively. "And if he hadn't, we'd be sorry," she adds, explaining that working was the same as breathing to her grandfather.

Although the family speaks of the premature loss of Stanley Buckman with subdued acceptance, this is in marked contrast to their suppression of the death of his younger son and Kathy's uncle, John. The tragic suicide has not been mitigated through discussion, and this omission has created a deep well of loss and sorrow in the hearts of the family. "We're not a very communicative family when it comes to such things," admits Kathy. "We talk business, and we joke, but when we gather as a family it's very low-key."

When controversy arises, the tension is typically eased by bringing in a family go-between. And the go-between for Bob Buckman's efforts to slow down Mertie's activities is his daughter, Kathy. "I'll get a call from Dad, and he'll let me know what's worrying him, then I'll call grandmother, saying, 'Grandmother, we have a problem,'" Kathy explains, with a grin that implies the exchange occurs with regularity. "And she'll ask, 'Who have you been talking to?' and I'll say,

'Someone who knows and cares about you,' and we go from there." This clashing of wills happens without direct confrontation, since abrasive confrontation is not Mertie's style. "Grandmother is soft-spoken and more likely to offer a carefully worded suggestion, rather than a command. She's rarely critical …she's much more likely to say nothing at all, rather than being outspoken about what is displeasing. When she is approving or offers praise, you can count on her being sincere."

There is one incident of direct confrontation in Kathy's memory, and she shakes her head with a grin as she recalls the very memorable incident. "I remember the time she was the angriest I've ever seen. It was when Dad moved in with her for a brief stay, following his divorce, and the two of them were [living] in the same house. Well, Dad decided it was time to redecorate. He took it upon himself to remove the light fixture in his old room—his bedroom when he was growing up—and then replaced it with recessed lighting. She was *furious*!" And did she express her displeasure by yelling at him? "Oh, no, she's always composed," Kathy chuckles, "but he's not!" She offers no elaboration.

Reflecting upon her grandmother as a role model, Kathy observes, "It's been interesting to know her, to watch her, over the years. She is a woman in her own right and is very independent, yet gracious. She became a powerfully influential person in a subtle feminine way, rather than in an aggressive masculine way."

Others who know Mertie also describe her in this way, as a woman who is quietly influential and possesses the power of deep inner strength. Brother Michael McGinniss observes that Mertie is a woman of power, yet her power is "worn lightly" and springs from her strength of character. "She is centered, she knows who she is, and she gives of herself from a sense of her connection with humanity and from the depths of herself," he says. Dr. Jim Daughdrill concurs that Mertie's power is derived from her strength of character. "It's hard to put into words, but Mertie has a quality of humility and piety—not the sappy kind, but the strong kind—that comes from selflessness. She is totally without self-consciousness, in that her work and influence are for the betterment of others, with very little investment of her own ego. That's the source of her power."

Brother Patrick O'Brien sums up Mertie's strength with great affection, "The granite of New Hampshire is part of her 'til death," he observes, quoting the Dartmouth alma mater anthem. The analogy is apropos to Mertie's "granite" strength, yet it is in contrast to the typical connotation of granite as cold, hard, or unyielding. Mertie's example of quiet strength is never intimidating, but one that inspires emulation. "The more you know Mertie, the more you want to live a selfless life," says Brother Pat. "She has taken the message of the Lord to 'Do unto others' to heart, and we are all the better for it."

Mertie's selfless application of the biblical Golden Rule for the betterment of society has established a pre-eminent precedent for Kathy Buckman Davis and other third-generation Buckmans. Fortunately for the younger generation following in their grandmother's footsteps, Mertie Buckman's life-long philanthropy has blazed a wide trail.

The Philanthropist

Pete Aviotti of Dunavant Development Company embraces Martie Buckman at the January 22, 1998, luncheon where it was announced that she would donate $1 million to the new Central Library in Memphis.
Photo: Copyright, 1998, *The Commercial Appeal,* Memphis, TN. Used with permission

Mertie W. Buckman's work is widespread, both in the Memphis community and beyond, yet there are some institutions with which her name is most associated. These organizations' missions are similar in their purpose to educate for the future of the community. Mertie's involvement with these groups over the years has gradually evolved into a focus on supporting educational opportunities for girls and women.

Associates point to Mertie as a "true" philanthropist: a woman who gives of herself, with a generosity prompted by values held dear. Mertie acknowledges that she derives a sense of meaning and direction from her philanthropic work. There is great satisfaction in giving, in making a difference. This is the lesson she has learned over decades of philanthropy, and this is the message she shares. It has become one of Mertie's missions to encourage philanthropy in others, particularly in women, who have not been the traditional "backbone" of fund-raising efforts.

Mertie's message is clear: It is important, even essential, for all of us to give to causes we care about, for the betterment of the entire community. Her appeal to the emergence of women as philanthropists is based upon this concept that giving is emotionally driven. Beth Dixon of the Community Foundation remarks on this emotional quality of Mertie's giving and the resulting sense of community instilled in other women. "Some benefactors may choose to make donations strategically, out of power motives, but Mertie's giving is out of her feeling that a project is meaningful and worthy," says Beth. Because Mertie chooses her causes with care, others are inspired by her giving and follow suit.

Beth recalls the Women in Philanthropy Steering Board's "Power of the Purse" educational event in March of 1995. Mertie was a speaker, along with "several wonderful women," including Barbara Hyde, Harry Mae Simons, Lynn Winbush, Honey Scheidt, and philanthropist Helen Hunt. "We had made arrangements to meet at the Racquet Club, and we had only so many seats. The luncheon was an immediate sell-out, but what was amazing was that we had calls from women all over the community who were pleading for tickets, just for a chance to hear Mertie speak," relates Beth. "They were yearning to hear her—she is held in very high esteem—and that is the moment when the Women's Foundation really 'took off.' We describe it as 'A Mertie Moment,' when the sheer magnetism of her presence inspired the camaraderie that will make this Foundation a powerful force in the community."

The Women's Foundation for a Greater Memphis

Although Mertie made the original gift of $50,000 to the "Women's Fund," as it was called in 1989, the Foundation itself was chartered in 1995. "It took some time to gather a community of women together to follow Mertie's lead and develop the vision of the Women's Foundation," Beth Dixon says. "We needed a board chair who could direct the efforts of a diverse group of women, who could inspire leadership, and who would provide a powerful example of women spearheading philanthropic efforts. Mertie knew who that woman should be—Barbara Hyde."

Beth was present when Mertie Buckman asked Barbara Hyde to chair the organization. "We went to lunch together at Aubergine's, and Mertie very simply appealed to Barbara to do this. She leaned over to Barbara at lunch, touched her lightly on the arm, and said, 'Barbara, we've got some work to do.'" Beth recalls the impact of the moment. "Barbara was awed, I think, and was powerfully influenced by Mertie's belief in this project," although at that time Barbara was rearing a very young child and committed to many community projects already underway. "But Barbara agreed, and the Foundation has taken off under her leadership. I'm sure, however, that there have been personal sacrifices along the way."

Barbara Hyde speaks of Mertie's influence and leadership with great admiration and gratitude for Mertie's mentoring. She had approached that first luncheon meeting with Mertie and Beth "girded to say 'no'" to heading the Foundation, due to the multitude of her other commitments. "But the truth is, I think any woman who cares about this city would find it impossible to say 'no' to Mertie," says Barbara. "She is such a quietly powerful presence that it would be unthinkable to turn down the opportunity to lend

Women's Foundation for a Greater Memphis
Executive Committee

Back Row(left to right):
    Beth Dixon, Executive Director
    Gayle Rose, Treasurer
    Amber Northcross
    Cassandra Webster, Vice Chair
    Debbie Binswanger
    Virginia Dunaway, former Executive Director

Front Row (left to right):
    Linda Kaplan
    Jennifer Satre, Chair
    Maxine Smith
    Dr. Indurani Tejwani, Secretary
Not pictured: Fredricka Hodges,
Barbara Hyde, and Becky West

support to a cause she finds important. And the work of the Women's Foundation is an important effort."

After assuming her role as chair of the Women's Foundation in 1995, Barbara has more than once expressed her gratitude to Mertie for encouraging her involvement. "This is the work that I feel most passionate about," she says, "and I am in Mertie's debt for her influence. She continues to be an inspiration to all of us, and I am privileged to think of her as a mentor in my work." Barbara describes the work of the Women's Foundation as a collaborative effort to empower women to impact the Memphis community through education, philanthropic effort, advocacy, and financial support of existing agencies. "But it is key to realize that by lifting up women we are lifting up all members of our community, women and men of diverse backgrounds and interests. If we empower all members of our community to be more economically self-sufficient and invested, then Memphis will make huge progress. The Women's Foundation is an effort to increase the available resources for the whole community—our mission is not about differently 'dividing the pie' of available resources, but it is about 'adding to the pie.'"

Barbara Hyde's vision for the Foundation is

Barbara Hyde and Mertie

reflected in the membership of its board of directors, composed of women from various backgrounds who are united in their common commitment. The unique quality of commitment that inspires the work of the Foundation was described by Beth Dixon. "At our first Development Committee meeting, there was a sense of inspired giving…even if it meant some sacrifice," she recalls thoughtfully. "It was a meeting that was memorably different from other meetings I've attended in my development work."

She offers in explanation that "men, who historically have been more in a position to direct foundations, tend to jockey for position. The pledges made may be a response to a challenge from another board member or a way to gain some status in the group. But this gathering of women was a time of communal giving from the heart. We went around the table and each made pledges according to her resources, without any comments like, 'I'll have to check with my husband'…," Beth relates. "It was an emotional moment, since all the women were so determined to see this happen. Then, when we got to Mertie, she pulled out her checkbook and said, 'Well, I'm a little short right now,' and we all burst into laughter! She wrote a check for a small amount—which actually wasn't that *small*—and later followed up on her pledge. She's a real joy, really 'one of the girls' with this group," Beth says with great admiration and affection.

In the Women's Foundation board room is a table called "Mertie's table." It was donated by a board member, Mickey Babcock, and is of beautifully distressed pine; around it are gathered twelve Queen Anne chairs. "The chairs are upholstered with African Kente cloth, donated by Fredricka Hodges, who also is on our board," Ellen Rolfes, immediate past executive director, points out. In the center of the table sits a woven African basket, donated by another board member, Kim Warnette. "This room symbolizes the coming together of women from different walks of life. It's a place where women gather and find a collective voice."

The work that takes place in this room is inspired and supported by Mertie. Ellen relates that Mertie recently had stopped by to bring her contribution to the annual fund. "She gave me a hug and a kiss on the cheek, and I know that this work is good work. Mertie brings the circle of women together...she *completes* the circle. When women come together, it's hard to separate them."

Young Women's Christian Association

Mertie Buckman is a long-time supporter of the Memphis Young Women's Christian Association (YWCA). It was there that she found friendships and purpose in her days as a newcomer to the city. She has served as a volunteer, as a representative to the

Mertie, an active volunteer for the YWCA since the late 1940s, was honored for her long service in 1982 by the renaming of the Raleigh YWCA as the Mertie Buckman Branch. Shown left to right following the dedication are the late Andrewnetta Hawkins-Jones, Mertie Buckman, Lila Beth Burke, and Helen Borland.
Photograph from personal collection of Mertie Buckman.

board of directors, and as president. To honor her contributions to the YWCA, the Raleigh Branch of the "YW" was named the Mertie Buckman Branch in 1982.

This organization's dedication to service through a hands-on grassroots approach is typical of Mertie Buckman's work. The mission of the YWCA is straightforward, and Mertie has found a common ground here, given that the values by which she lives, including religious tolerance and the elimination of racism, are articulated in the organization's mission statement: "Strengthened by diversity the Association draws together members who strive to create opportunities for women's growth, leadership, and power in order to attain a common vision: peace, justice, freedom, and dignity for all people."

The administrative headquarters on Highland Street are pleasant yet functional; the atmosphere is one of women at serious work among friends. The office's tables hold brochures outlining YWCA programs, including child care, afterschool care, and scheduled classes for children and adults in swimming, gymnastics, tennis, guitar, violin, and watercolor painting. The "YW" offers extensive services for abused women, including two emergency shelters, and operates a day-activity center for mentally retarded women. Educational programs target employment training, breast-cancer detection, and youth leadership.

Mertie Buckman, supporter of the YWCA's work since her first days in Memphis in the the late 1940s, was photographed in December, 1996, with other YWCA board past-presidents and a former executive director. Shown in the front row, from left, are Lanetha Branch, Mertie, Ellida Fri, and former executive director Lila Beth Burke. In the second row, from left, are Sally Johnson, Susan Goldsmith, Inetta F. Rogers, Donna Sue Shannon, Agnes Pokrandt, and Donna Fisher.
Photograph courtesy of the YWCA, Memphis.

On a wall in the boardroom hangs a photograph of Mertie Buckman, taken at the time of her presidency; her attractive face radiates with calm self-confidence. Gesturing toward the framed photograph, Michelle Fowlkes, recently appointed executive director, smiles and says, "When I think of her, I always remember her on her knees in the garden, planting flowers at the Mertie Buckman Branch. That's how we think of her, because Mertie's always been one of us."

Girls, Incorporated

In October of 1997, Girls, Incorporated, of Memphis received a one-million-dollar endowment from Mertie Buckman. The announcement was made at the opening ceremony for the newly renovated and expanded Lucille Devore Tucker Center, Mertie Buckman Wing, on North Seventh in Memphis. At the opening, a large gathering of girls, dressed in white dresses and smiling with excitement, sang the popular song, *I Believe I Can Fly*, in tribute to Mertie Buckman. She responded with a brief speech, proclaiming the occasion as a "wonderful, wonderful day." She was then given a personal tour of the completed building, which she already knew well from poring over blueprints before construction began.

"Mertie is an inspiration to us and to our board," says Patricia Howard, executive director of Girls, Incorporated "She has challenged us to plan well and

to be accountable. She's said to us more than once, 'Come back and talk to me when your plans are more firm,' and we've done that. Mertie's financial support is evidence that we're doing a good job at what we do—educating girls to take charge of their futures."

Girls, Incorporated, is an organization which has been reaching out to young girls since 1946. According to Patricia Howard, the organization's full-time staff of 35 serves 3,500 girls a year. The majority of girls who participate in programs or receive services are from African-American families with annual incomes of less than $15,000.

The central offices of Girls, Incorporated, on Beale Street, are in a walk-up office suite overlooking the popular tourist attractions of blues clubs and cafés. The colorfully decorated offices are cheerful and welcoming. Available throughout the office is the organization's literature, edged with the boldfaced slogan: **"GIRLS CAN DO."** And the group's offered programs send the same message. Through Girls, Incorporated, girls may learn about careers and life skills, health and sexuality, leadership and community action, sports, and culture and heritage. An Educational Opportunity Center offers counseling and technical assistance for continuing education and training. A Life Skills Education Center targets adolescents' decision-making about pregnancy prevention and career planning. Girls, Incorporated, also works with the Memphis City Schools through their Educational Talent Search, designed to encourage continued education and career planning.

Patricia Howard speaks of the organization's programs with pride mixed with concern. "It's been difficult at times to raise enough funds to continue and expand our work. Mertie's been a wonderful example to the community concerning our need for financial support," she says, noting that she and Mertie have discussed often the necessity to encourage women, in particular, to give of their money. "Traditionally, women have given of their time, and men have had control of financial giving. Most women don't yet think of financial giving as a responsibility, and some women think they have to be lucky enough to have a windfall before they can make a difference," observes Patricia. "But Mertie is outspoken about this; she asks, 'How can you *not* give? If we don't take care of these girls, who will?' It's a powerful message: this *must* be done."

In October of 1997, Mertie, shown with two young members of Girls, Incorporated, was on hand for the opening ceremony for the renovated and expanded Lucille Devore Tucker Center, Mertie Buckman Wing, on North Seventh in Memphis. Members of Girls, Incorporated, sang the popular song, I Believe I Can Fly, *in tribute to Mertie, whose endowment to Girls, Incorporated of $1 million had just been announced.*
Photograph courtesy of the YWCA, Memphis.

Rhodes College

Buckman Hall —Rhodes College, Memphis
Photograph courtesy of Rhodes College, Memphis.

Rhodes College sits on an expanse of beautifully landscaped acreage just minutes from the international headquarters of Buckman Laboratories. The collegiate Gothic architecture is a tangible reminder of the college's founding in 1837 and its long affiliation with the Presbyterian church. The school's traditional facade also speaks of Rhodes' long-standing commitment to excellence in liberal arts education. Rhodes instills in its students the traditional values Mertie holds dear from her own educational experiences: excellence, high achievement, honor, responsibility, and stewardship.

The association between the Buckman family and Rhodes College is long. Both Dr. Buckman and Mrs. Buckman have served on the board of trustees, with Mertie serving on the board from 1983 until 1997. Her many years of annual support to the college have been supplemented by additional gifts that funded the endowed Mertie W. Buckman International Internship Program, Buckman Hall, the renovation of the Burrow Library, the Mertie Willigar and Stanley J. Buckman Scholarship, the Mertie Willigar Buckman Chair of International Studies, and the P. K. Seidman Fellow in International Political Economy.

Rhodes College awarded Mertie an honorary Doctor of Humane Letters degree in May of 1991 to honor her strength of character, her sharp mind, her leadership, and her love for Rhodes. "Mertie's giving spirit is like the rising level of the sea that raises all boats," says President James Daughdrill. "When we reflect upon her contributions and her character, she brings us all to a new level." He notes that, although Mertie has announced her resignation from the college's board, she continues to sit on the advisory council to the Margaret Hyde Society, which targets educational opportunities for women. "Mertie is gentle, but never passive; she's tough and full of gusto, but sensitive; and she balances independence with real humility. I can't imagine being asked to describe anyone else and using so many superlatives. We have all benefited from knowing her, and those who don't know her have missed out on something truly special."

Rhodes College's President Dr. James Daughdrill (left) and Chancellor David Harlow (right) were photographed with Dr. Mertie Buckman in 1996, five years after the college awarded her an honorary Doctor of Humane Letters degree in recognition of "her strength of character, her sharp mind, her leadership, and her love of Rhodes."
Photograph courtesy of Rhodes College, Memphis

Following the 1990 groundbreaking and dedicatory ceremony for the new Buckman Hall at Rhodes College, President James Daughdrill commends the generosity of Mertie Buckman.
Photograph courtesy of Rhodes College, Memphis.

Right:
Mertie Buckman (center), with shovel in hand, prepares for the groundbreaking and dedication of Buckman Hall at Rhodes College in 1990.
Photograph courtesy of Rhodes College, Memphis.

Christian Brothers University

The name Mertie Buckman is well known on the Christian Brothers University (CBU) campus, and both students and alumni readily acknowledge her long years of contributions and service. Christian Brothers University is a private, co-educational Catholic university founded by a religious order, the Christian Brothers, dedicated to outstanding education through its mission to educate the poor. "I think Mertie likes that about us—our mission to serve the poor and underprivileged," says Brother Patrick O'Brien, a development director for the university. In describing the loyalty Mertie has shown to the school over the years, he says, "She has a similar focus to help the underprivileged, and Mertie knows how hard teaching really is."

In 1988, Mertie made a gift to CBU for the development and landscaping of Buckman Quad, an outdoor campus center where students congregate in natural surroundings. Her subsequent gifts have been used to build Buckman Hall, to establish the student Scholarship Initiative, and to support the Theodore Drahmann Scholarship Fund, the Campus Improvement Fund, the Visual Arts Fund, and the Annual Fund. Mertie has served on the board of trustees since 1988 and has been active on many CBU committees: the President's Council, the Religious Affairs Committee, the Building and Grounds Committee, and the Visual Arts Committee.

"Mertie's total contributions to us at this point are over five million dollars," Brother Pat relates. "In addition to her financial contributions, she serves tirelessly: attending meetings, offering suggestions, and accompanying me to make requests of other donors. She follows up on her donations and doesn't hesitate to ask others to do the same. It's a tremendous asset to the university to have her support, and we also care deeply for her. Our former president, Brother Theodore, would call her 'Saint Mertie,'" he says, smiling affectionately, then adds, "We wanted to acknowledge Mertie in some meaningful way, so we proposed erecting a statue in her honor. She agreed, and sculptress Jill Burkee was commissioned to do the work."

Unveiled in 1993, the marble bas-relief sculpture entitled *The Essence of Mertie* is inside Buckman Hall at the university. The impressive sculpture was rendered in Carrara marble, taken from the Italian quarry once used by the legendary High Renaissance artist Michelangelo. According to Jill Burkee, the sculpture is a depiction of the spirit of harmony and generosity that Mertie Buckman brings to various aspects of the university community. The image of Mertie is the central figure, seated and holding flowers, and she is surrounded by representative figures for various components of education at Christian Brothers: the schools housed in Buckman Hall, the geographical and cultural diversity of students at the university, the basic natural elements, the importance of communication, and the search for knowledge.

Mertie Buckman, who has served on the board of trustees of Christian Brothers University since 1988, was the featured speaker for the dedication of Buckman Hall at CBU in 1997. In addition to her initial gift in 1988 for the development and landscaping of Buckman Quad, subsequent gifts have been used to build Buckman Hall, to establish the student Scholarship Initiative, and to support the Theodore Drahmann Scholarship Fund, the Campus Improvement Fund , the Visual Arts Fund, and the Annual Fund.
Photograph courtesy of CBU, Memphis.

The process of commissioning the work and seeing it installed was a long one, and Mertie speaks with great affection of the relationship forged with the young artist, Jill Burkee, during those days of planning and preparation. "She's a wonderful person," Mertie says with admiration. Mertie is fond of recalling her trip to Pietrasanta, Italy, to see the Carrara marble lifted out of the quarry, as well as her earlier trips to Jill's New York studio.

"There was a special affinity between the two, Jill and Mertie," says Brother Michael McGinniss, who accompanied both to dinner during one of their visits at the Russian Tea Room in New York City. "Perhaps it was the creative spirit that both share, or perhaps it was their international experiences, but whatever may be the explanation, there was a bond there…almost a spiritual mentoring."

Jill Burkee, who won recognition from the National Sculpture Society for *The Essence of Mertie*, speaks of Mertie's impact upon her. "Mertie's simplicity demands that I use few words. It is hard to explain, but to go on and on somehow takes away from her elegance." During their first meeting, Jill realized that she "was in the company of an incredible woman," and her impression was reinforced later during the

In her studio, Sculptress Jill Burkee (left) relates the significance of the 12 youthful figures being sculpted in 1992 as part of the marble bas-relief sculpture featuring Mertie Buckman, The Essence of Mertie. *The sculpture was commissioned by Christian Brother University for placement in Buckman Hall.*

Photograph from personal collection of Mertie Buckman.

Russian Tea Room dinner described by Brother Michael McGinniss. "We were enjoying a wonderful meal," she recalls, "and someone mentioned that Mertie and I were alike in some way. For me it was one of the greatest compliments of my lifetime. Mertie, in her quiet, poignant manner responded, saying that 'Neither of us try to be more than who we are.' I will never forget the feeling of being so generously welcomed to the side of such a wonderful human being with such piercing, honest simplicity."

Reflecting upon the creative process as she labored to create *The Essence of Mertie*, Jill confesses to moments of elusive inspiration and self-doubt, when she felt "overcome…adrift in confusion." At such times, she called upon memories of Mertie's "humble dignity" and the instantaneous spiritual bonding between them, and Jill was once again imbued with inspired confidence. "Mertie is one of those rare beacons in life…reminding me that the shore is always near if I remain true to myself."

That thought succinctly sums up what is perhaps Mertie Buckman's greatest gift, intrinsic and beyond monetary value: A quietly inspiring presence shining as a rare beacon in life.

Life's Lessons

What does life teach, when one is blessed with insight as well as longevity? Mertie is not given to philosophical bents, but she thoughtfully reflects upon the reality that life's lessons continue past the markers of early adulthood. Our culture celebrates youth, and the prospect of aging is a foreign—even frightening—one in such a culture. Yet the experience of aging with integrity, rather than despair, is an invaluable experience to share.

"I am not a person to idealize," Mertie warns pragmatically. "You learn to let go of what you must, and you find that life goes on. It is time for change, and you can find new ways to enjoy life and to make a difference."

Mertie has had in her life many such times for change: the loss of her parents, the abrupt transition into widowhood, the loss of her son, and the staggering challenge of guiding a company after its loss of its leading "giant of a man," Dr. Stanley Buckman. Mertie vividly recalls her feelings after

In 1997, Mertie was the recipient of a medal of excellence from the Mississippi University for Women in Columbus.
Photograph from personal collection of Mertie Buckman.

losing her husband and her time of mourning and varying degrees of self-doubt. "It's hard, and I'm not sure it would be any easier to have any warning about loss," she reflects. There are, however, rare moments of reconciliation to personal loss. "I remember there was a woman, who lived in Arkansas—in Fayetteville—who was married to a man who had been a [Buckman Laboratories] company employee. After Stanley's death, she invited me to come for a visit. I went, and it was good to go. I was so grateful to her. It was the first time that I had traveled since he had died. And I had traveled alone before, of course, but somehow it was different after Stanley died. You can become dependent...I had been home alone and, after the trip to Arkansas, I realized, 'Well, you don't have to just sit home.' You know, you can easily get into a rut. It was such a nice thing for her to do, to invite me to visit like that. I realized that life doesn't stop," she says.

And the lure of life's rich experiences has never "stopped" for Mertie, as she has continued since Stanley Buckman's death 20 years ago to travel extensively and maintain her own household. She has become increasingly independent over the years, but she enjoys companionship; there have been times, particularly while she was recovering from a hip replacement, when a friend has moved in briefly to assist her. "She's a good companion," she says of the woman.

Mertie has built a life of many interests, close family, and good companions who have stood by her through the years. She is a spiritual woman, but she does not speak of her private faith. Her support of her church and other church-related institutions attests to her Christian beliefs, and she is an elder *emerita* of the Raleigh Presbyterian Church.

One of the most valuable lessons taught to Mertie in mid-life was the obtaining of spiritual comfort by sharing her feelings of personal loss with other women, who also had experienced similar grief. She has shared her private feelings with a few trusted friends, and she often speaks with deep emotion of the importance of staying connected to people throughout life—especially during the hard times.

Mertie also believes connection transcends divorce, which should not negate the value of maintaining relationships. "I think it [the divorce process and upheaval] is a hard time, but you have to accept your children's decisions. You can't control others. You can't assign blame...if you do, you get all tangled up in your emotions," she observes. "I remember not long after Bob's ex-wife, Miriam, remarried, she moved out to California." Miriam, the mother of her granddaughters, Kathy and Margaret, and her grandson, Karl, lost her new husband when he died suddenly of a heart attack. "I went out to California for the funeral, and some were surprised that I went to the funeral since Bob and Miriam were divorced, and this was the man who had married his ex-wife. But I felt it was right to go...I went for the children's sakes. It was a hard time for them, and they were worried about their mother. It was important to go, to keep connected with them, and to support the children."

Mertie's commitment to her family is obvious as she reflects upon her experience as a wife and mother. She was loyal to her husband and dearly loved him, even when they disagreed. Considering Dr. Buckman's dedicated focus on his work, it is likely that Mertie spent most of her time single-handedly managing the household, rearing their two sons, and pursuing her own outside interests; yet she took her role as wife seriously and generally put her husband's interests ahead of her own. "I remember once when I wanted to go on a trip to South America. I mentioned it to Stanley...and he never said I *couldn't* do anything...but he just said that he didn't want me to leave right then. So, I didn't go. It was unusual for him to object, and I thought, 'Why fuss? What's the point?' If he needed me to be there then, I knew I could always go [to South America] later," she says, giving a prime example of her diplomatic patience and adaptability.

This is Mertie's way, to consider the wishes of others without losing her sense of herself in the process. She speaks briefly of the need for husbands and wives to develop the art of pleasing each other, without losing sight of themselves. "We have to remember that we need other people," she says softly. Somehow, Mertie created the balance necessary to assume independence, to know herself and "stand her ground" when necessary, and to value her connection to those she loves. This ability to be separate, yet connected, is truly an accomplishment which demands a firm sense of self. It is only when we are confident in *who we are* that we are able to share relationships that are interdependent, rather than dependent.

Thus, when conflict arises in relationships, Mertie rarely will become involved in an outright argument. She's more likely to comment, "What's the point?" Her philosophy, formed over most of this century, is that "sometimes wives have to find a way to get around their husbands" and manage disagreement with diplomacy and patience.

This same diplomacy and patience were employed in the rearing of her two sons—she prefers subtle-but-firm influence and resists insistence. She says simply that she reared her boys with respect for their differences as individuals and with a certainty that they would find their own way. She recalls her days rearing Bob and John with fondness, describing the boys' antics and their rambunctious school days. "They would need some calming down late in the afternoon, and I'd sit them down so we could read together or listen to a little radio. We'd get involved in some project—like building the tree house—and they'd settle down," she smiles. Mertie's fondness for her children and her grandchildren is evident in her musings, and she knows the value of early educational experiences for children.

When she is reminded that Bob remembers her reading to him, especially a favorite book entitled *Chippy Bobby*, she is surprised and pleased. She vaguely recalls the book, but she mentions that her grandson, Karl, also remembers her reading to him. "He'll ask me, 'Do you still have such-and-such book, Grandmother?' I don't remember it, but *he* does," she laughs, adding that children well remember their early learning.

What about her mid-life years? Did she ever experience the "empty nest" syndrome and was it difficult to let go when her sons left home? Mertie chuckles and shakes her head. "No. When Bob left to go to Purdue, and [later] John went to Illinois, I knew it was time for them to grow…to go on. We mothers have to hold [ourselves] back sometimes to let go. You don't want them to stay at home, to be dependent. You want them to be independent," she observes sagely.

Mertie speaks of some worries she has about her grandchildren or great-grandchildren, some problems in their schools, and her underlying sense of frustration that she cannot make some things easier for them. But she does not interfere or intrude, and she has "no regrets." When reminded that her granddaughter Kathy has related that she "argues" with her grandmother about trips to the lake and Kathy's boating alone, Mertie retorts, "I wouldn't call it an argument. Kathy's always going off on her own. I remember she [participated in] an Outward Bound program and told me about camping out in the rain alone in a tent," she relates, shaking her head. "I think I would have wanted someone with me, but I've never had much experience in camping. I remember the girls' camps in Vermont, when I was growing up. The city girls would come for the summer to camp, and I was always so envious of them," Mertie recalls wistfully. But this train of thought is not pursued, and Mertie returns her thoughts to her experience of motherhood.

"I did my best as a mother, and I am proud of my family," she says. Mertie, who has devoted her later life to championing women's issues, has only sons. Did she ever wish for a daughter? "No, but I enjoy my granddaughters," she laughs. "Girls and boys are different. My boys were pretty straightforward. I knew what they were thinking, what worried them. Girls are harder to know; sometimes they don't come straight out and say what's bothering them."

This is just one of the many observations Mertie has made concerning the differences between boys and girls, between men and women. She has lived through a century which has brought definitive changes in the status of women, and she moves in primarily male-dominated circles in which, historically, few women have had access. Even in her civic activities, most of her memberships are on boards of directors that are predominantly male. She has, indeed, served as a trailblazer in changing (if not eliminating) gender bias. "Other people have said that to me," she acknowledges, "but I don't really think of it that way. I just do what I do." It is characteristic of Mertie to deprecate her trailblazer status and to think of herself as just doing her work.

Mertie Buckman is, however, well aware of the need for women to be recognized, educated, and encouraged in their achievements. She recalls again her family story of her grandfather's refusal to support his daughter's wish for higher education. "Women traditionally have been shortchanged," she states knowingly. "Sometimes they are not held in high regard.

Even today, you can see it in certain cultures—in some immigrant families, for instance—where the boys are sent to school but not the girls. Women must be recognized for their abilities," Mertie emphasizes in a strong and determined voice.

The Mertie Buckman in her young-matron years, when Stanley Buckman ruled the Buckman Laboratories with a firm hand, gave little evidence of the calmly outspoken and independent elder citizen she has become. Her long-time friend Alma Pierotti spoke of Mertie's later accomplishments with surprised admiration, as did Rhodes' Jim Daughdrill. "We had no inkling of her wit or her ability," Jim observes thoughtfully. Mertie's abilities were always there, but it's reasonable to assume that her quiet, understated style was eclipsed by her husband's more extroverted style. The tendencies of women to serve as facilitators and to defer to those who command in a more aggressive style contribute to their being ostensibly "overlooked," but in overlooking women's abilities the community loses invaluable resources.

Mertie points out that she has been in groups and committee meetings where women fail to speak their minds or voice objections to the business at hand. "I suppose it's just habit," she muses, "but we need to develop the confidence to do just that: to *speak up*. Women have a great deal to offer, and we need to look to each other for encouragement, for support."

She mentions that she has spoken recently with Angie Gardner, director of development for St. Mary's, who told her that girls' schools typically receive substantially fewer dollars from alumnae than do boys' schools. "Can you *believe* this?" Mertie asks in astonishment. "It's not right."

Mertie puts her knowledge of gender inequities to good use as an outspoken—although soft-spoken—advocate for equal appreciation of women's abilities. Her good friend Dora Ivey refers to Mertie's activism for women by relating a story of Mertie's speech at the Memphis Rotary Club in 1996. Mertie was awarded the Rotary Club's Community Service Award for that year, and in accepting it gave a most memorable address. "She thanked the members for their congratulations," Dora recalls, "and then she said, 'And I want to congratulate you on finally allowing women memberships in your organization.'" Dora related that Mertie admonished the members for waiting until it was no longer an option, but a requirement, that they do so. Dora appreciates Mertie's way of getting to the heart of any issue.

Mertie also remembers a Rotary Club reception for new members when her friend Judy Drescher, director of the Memphis and Shelby County Libraries, was being welcomed into membership along with other—all male—new members. "There was a receiving line to shake hands with new members, and Judy was being overlooked. The men would shake hands with other men and simply not notice her. So, Judy just moved herself up in the line, in order to get noticed," Mertie says, telling this story with a brief shake of her head. "People will often look to men in suits as the people to know, and they will overlook women, without even being aware of it."

Having become aware long ago that females receive short-shrift in higher education, Mertie has become a well-known champion of education for girls and women. This has been the focus of her philanthropic efforts for years, and she is adamant about

the need for girls to "know what they need to know…in particular, girls need to know the facts of life," she states firmly. "It's just ridiculous to allow a girl to grow up and not know how to prevent pregnancy. It's as bad as not knowing the basic facts of biology on your wedding night. You have to know in order to make good choices. It's just basic common sense, and it's ridiculous to keep knowledge from young people. It's a denial of the basic facts of life."

Mertie experiences frustration with "foolishness," so she has firm opinions on the importance of living in a greater community that protects and supports individual rights and responsibilities. Although she has only rarely become involved in politics, she and her husband were outspoken supporters of Mayor Edmund Orgill's bid for the city mayor's position after the death of Memphis politico Edward Hull "Boss" Crump.

"I remember going to vote in those years," Mertie reminisces. "And some people would say that they hadn't even bothered to vote, that they were sure Mr. Crump knew what was best for them," she says with some disbelief. "I know some people thought of him as a 'benevolent dictator' of sorts, but people can't just give away their power like that. It makes you vulnerable. I always asked myself, 'What if the next 'dictator' isn't so good?'"

As a long-time community activist, Mertie Buckman has witnessed the city's struggle with racism. She has quietly modeled an attitude toward inclusiveness, especially in her work with the YWCA. She remembers working at the "YW" with the wife of the new president of LeMoyne-Owen College in the early 1960s. "I remember Mrs. Walker saying that if it hadn't been for our meetings and luncheons at the 'YW,' she would have felt lost in the city." In those days before the Civil Rights Act of 1964 brought racial desegregation to the country, white women and black women did not "mix," and Mertie admits that integrated meetings were a learning experience for the community. "First we learned to gather together for afternoon meetings, then to eat together," she recalls. She also remembers the example of one of her role models, Ethel Niermeyer, a long-time executive director of the YWCA. "She was a great influence and a good woman. She had taught briefly in Turkey in her early years, so she was something of a pioneer herself." The early example of the YWCA in rejecting attitudes of racism continues today in its mission and outreach programs.

Mertie's spirit of inclusiveness and of celebrating diversity is evident in her varied friendships, in her work with the alliance of diverse women at the Women's Foundation, and even in her casual conversation about traveling to and reading about other cultures. She models religious tolerance in her support of varied church-related organizations and in her membership in the National Conference of Christians and Jews. She has no qualms about appreciating cultural attitudes differing from her own and values the insight gained by considering other points of view. Her openness to cultural insights is illustrated by her story of a recent trip to visit her granddaughter Margaret in Santa Fe. "Margaret's new home is near an American Indian burial ground, and they say there is a spirit living in the house," she relates with enthusiasm. "But it's a good spirit…very kind," she adds.

Her appreciation for myth, history, and for things not yet understood contributes a vibrancy to Mertie's essence that belies her status as a nonagenarian. "I'm never bored, but the time for dancing is past, I'm afraid," she laughs. Although Mertie has lost treasured relationships over the years—most recently her best friend, Jane Himes, who has joined her family in Texas because of illness—she continues to relish both old and new friendships, and her many interests remain active and eagerly embraced.

As she approaches her ninety-fourth natal day, it is still difficult for Mertie to give in to the demands of aging. "It is frustrating," she admits, "to have to slow down." She seems to accept this physical curtailment with characteristic pragmatism. "It's time now," she observes matter-of-factly, "to let go of some of my obligations."

Even after she passes the torch of civic activism to other capable hands, Mertie's far-sighted vision and commitment to shaping her world into a better place than she found will continue to inspire and influence philanthropy in Memphis and the surrounding area. Far into the new millennium, now poised upon civilization's threshhold, will be felt the impact of this life well lived and of the future leaders touched and influenced by the essence of Mertie.

Epilogue

As interviews were recorded during 1997 for this brief biography of Mertie Willigar Buckman, community awards and honors continued to accrue to this First Lady of Philanthropy. Last October, she was named one of the 50 Outstanding Women of the Mid-South by *Women's News of the Mid-South* and was an honoree at the awards dinner.

At Mertie's table were seated her son, Bob, and his wife, Joyce, and Bob's daughter, Kathy, and a handful of colleagues. The family dynamics are similar to those in most family units. Bob teases his mother about his medical checkup that afternoon, saying that his physician "spent about 20 minutes checking me out and about 30 minutes asking about you!" They laugh and joke about who should pay the medical bill, then the conversation veers away from "average" family dynamics as Mertie asks her son about the latest happenings at the family business, Buckman Laboratories. It is clear that mother and son, as well as granddaughter Kathy, speak the same language. Not until the evening's speaker begins her after-dinner address is there another flash of "normal" family dynamics. Bob makes some comment to the woman seated next to him, then Mertie leans over to whisper reprovingly to her son, who nods his head and maintains a respectful silence. Even when a son has wealth and power and is chairman of the board of Buckman Laboratories, he is subject to his mother's wishes.

Following dinner, Mertie's granddaughter, Kathy Buckman Davis, is asked what it's like to be a part of a family known for wealth and influence. She hesitates, then admits that her few years with her own legal practice in Atlanta before joining the family business in Memphis allowed her some anonymity that was unique and refreshing. "I have a hard time thinking of Grandmother as a woman of a certain mystique in this town. I sometimes have to be reminded that people who may appear to be kind and solicitous may have other agendas," she says reflectively.

In a society which equates money with power and status, the allure of that power can erect barriers between people and, in some cases, invite intrusion from others. An executive assistant to an influential college president comments that she admires Mrs. Buckman for her kindness and her impeccable manners. "She is a true lady, *really* a lady," she says with emphasis, conjuring up the image of the genteel lady of the Old South. "She's so gracious that I sometimes feel sorry for her, because people are always after her for money," she sighs sympathetically.

Similar comments created a recurrent theme during the year of interviewing friends and colleagues of Mertie Buckman, and one wonders how she remains unscathed by the exploitive greed, either blatant or covert, constantly hovering at her shoulder? An equally perplexing question is how she escaped the lure of status and power that others seek or may consider her "due" and privilege? However she accomplished it, she has completely eluded the snares of elitism, egotism, arrogance, and self-aggrandizement.

Perhaps Mertie's secret weapon against psychological snares is her strong sense of self and her "comfort within her own skin"; she has always been and remains a self-contained, authentic individual. A spiritual teaching comes to mind—"the soul without evil does not recognize nor is tempted by evil"—but that speaks to but one facet of Mertie's integrity.

Perhaps Mertie offered her own authentication when she told sculptress Jill Burkee that "neither of us try to be more than who we are." Or perhaps Jill shone light on the mystery of Mertie's essence when she described her as "one of those rare beacons in life" offering faith in and affirmation of human worth. Each person who has come under the influence of Mertie Willigar Buckman will have his or her own impression of what comprises her greatest gift...and that is the elusive, mysterious essence of Mertie.

Trish Calvert, Ph.D., is a psychologist in private practice in Germantown, Tennessee. A former newspaper columnist and professor of psychology, she divides her time among her practice, consulting in business and academic settings, and rearing two children.

Ilene Jones~Cornwell, former publications writer and editor for the Tennessee Historical Commission and Vanderbilt University Medical Center, operates an editorial and typesetting firm, Typography 2000, in Nashville. She has produced four volumes spanning 1901-1991 in the *Biographical Directory of the Tennessee General Assembly* series and has served as editor for 35 writers since 1970.